Marketing the 21st Century Library

The Time Is Now

Debra Lucas-Alfieri

AMSTERDAM • BOSTON • CAMBRIDGE • HEIDELBERG
LONDON • NEW YORK • OXFORD • PARIS • SAN DIEGO
SAN FRANCISCO • SINGAPORE • SYDNEY • TOKYO
Chandos Publishing is an imprint of Elsevier

Acquiring Editor: George Knott
Editorial Project Manager: Harriet Clayton
Project Manager: Preethy J Mampally
Designer: Mark Rogers

Chandos Publishing is an imprint of Elsevier
225 Wyman Street, Waltham, MA 02451, USA
Langford Lane, Kidlington, OX5 1GB, UK

© D. Lucas-Alfieri, 2015. All rights reserved.

No part of this publication may be reproduced or transmitted in any form or by any means, electronic or mechanical, including photocopying, recording, or any information storage and retrieval system, without permission in writing from the publisher. Details on how to seek permission, further information about the Publisher's permissions policies and our arrangements with organizations such as the Copyright Clearance Center and the Copyright Licensing Agency, can be found at our website: www.elsevier.com/permissions.

This book and the individual contributions contained in it are protected under copyright by the Publisher (other than as may be noted herein).

Notices
Knowledge and best practice in this field are constantly changing. As new research and experience broaden our understanding, changes in research methods, professional practices, or medical treatment may become necessary.

Practitioners and researchers must always rely on their own experience and knowledge in evaluating and using any information, methods, compounds, or experiments described herein. In using such information or methods they should be mindful of their own safety and the safety of others, including parties for whom they have a professional responsibility.

To the fullest extent of the law, neither the Publisher nor the authors, contributors, or editors, assume any liability for any injury and/or damage to persons or property as a matter of products liability, negligence or otherwise, or from any use or operation of any methods, products, instructions, or ideas contained in the material herein.

British Library Cataloguing in Publication Data
A catalogue record for this book is available from the British Library

Library of Congress Cataloging-in-Publication Data
A catalog record for this book is available from the Library of Congress

Library of Congress Control Number: 2015940172

ISBN 978-1-84334-773-6

For information on all Chandos Publishing
visit our website at http://store.elsevier.com/

Printed and bound in the United Kingdom

Marketing the 21st Century Library

Contents

Author's introduction   ix
Acknowledgements   xiii

1 Introduction   1
    1.1 Introduction   1
    1.2 Early definitions of marketing   3
    1.3 The profession: A super-marketing experience   4

2 From the past to the future: Library as place   7
    2.1 Marketing in necessity   9
    2.2 Marketing libraries in the past   9
    2.3 Samuel Sweet Green   10
    2.4 John Cotton Dana   10
    2.5 S.R. Ranganathan   13
    2.6 Francis K.W. Drury   13
    2.7 Early academic marketing steps   14
    2.8 The future   15
    2.9 Librarians of the future offer full-text delivery seamlessly   16
    2.10 Conclusion   17
    2.11 Discussion questions   17
    References   18

3 Marketing plan research and assessment   19
    3.1 Using quantitative and qualitative data   21
    3.2 Using action research   22
    3.3 Assessment tools   23
    3.4 Avoiding assessment challenges   28
    3.5 IRB process   29
    3.6 Conclusion   29
    3.7 Review questions   29
    References   30

4 Creating the marketing plan   31
    4.1 Introduction   31
    4.2 Components of a market plan for the academic library   34
    4.3 Conclusion   38
    4.4 Exercises   38
    References   38

5	**Project control—Managing marketing initiatives**		**41**
	5.1	Introduction	41
	5.2	Taming a potential beast	43
	5.3	The unexpected turns: Change management	46
	5.4	Discussion questions	48
	5.5	A library's tale—Case study	48
	5.6	Practice case study questions	49
		References	49
6	**Partnerships**		**51**
	6.1	Partnership opportunities and constituencies (POC—Pronounced "poke")	51
	6.2	From constituents to partners—Forging the way	52
	6.3	POC—Faculty	57
	6.4	POC and administrative or inter- and-intradepartmental partnerships	61
	6.5	Community involvement	64
	6.6	Conclusion	65
	6.7	Discussion questions	66
		References	66
7	**Resources and services to promote**		**67**
	7.1	Market first, promote last	67
	7.2	Histories of our leading competition—Easier-to-use resources	68
	7.3	Marketing what sets us apart	69
	7.4	Customer service	70
	7.5	Embedding librarians into campus life	71
	7.6	Communications	71
	7.7	Discussion questions	73
		References	73
8	**Using technology to market and promote**		**75**
	8.1	Introduction	75
	8.2	Social medium	77
	8.3	Twitter	78
	8.4	Pinterest	78
	8.5	Online games	79
	8.6	Library Web sites	79
	8.7	Web sites vs mobile apps	81
	8.8	Facebook	82
	8.9	Discussion questions	83
		References	84

9	Marketing a profession: Marketing the future	85
	9.1 Introduction	85
	9.2 The time is now. Marketing the profession: If we wait it will be too late	85
	9.3 Future of marketing libraries and the profession—If we wait, it will be too late	86
	9.4 Customer service	88
	9.5 Mission, vision, and SWOT analysis (Think)	90
	9.6 Assessment and planning (TIPR: Investigate and plan)	91
	9.7 Form partnerships (TIPR: React)	91
	9.8 Promote the five W's	92
	9.9 Conclusion	93
	9.10 Exercises	94
	References	94

Conclusion 95
Suggested readings 97
Index 101

Author's introduction

"So, what are you doing for a living now?" my high school friend asked at my 25th high school reunion.

"I'm a college librarian," I proudly replied.

"Well, I guess they won't need you much longer, will they?" he joked. Seriously.

That's when it hit me: the profession is at a crossroad. As such, so too is the library. Well, if the profession does not respond to these unfortunate but common remarks, who will?

I'm what you might call an "unlikely librarian." I was the high school student that is remembered for being voted the "Wildest Senior." I was a dreamer, who could be found feeding ducks at the park on sunny days when I belonged in my vocational shop class. I wasn't even sure how to find my high school library! Defiantly, I'd question authority and challenge the teachers to challenge me. Years have passed, and here I am, defending the existence what should be the core of academic institutions: the academic library. I am here to defend its existence, rally troops, and provide directions along the way. Knowledge is power, and it is time we take what we know and lead our profession from the brink of disillusionment to fulfillment.

I love the profession and the institution. It's the academics that I hold most closely to my heart. It is the college librarian who trains future health-care workers, communications specialists, engineers, politicians, activists, and educators to pave the way forward with the love for the information that leads to knowledge. The future of generations. We can install a love for knowledge, a love for evaluating knowledge, and a love for sharing that knowledge with every person with whom we interact: our constituents. I know I'm speaking in existential terms, but to save our profession, we need to expand our current modus operandi.

Librarians are married to libraries. There can be no divorce. But there can be a certain death without a proactively planned approach to saving the institution of knowledge management and display, otherwise known of as the "library." The marriage of library to librarian should produce societal knowledge. A "brain child" so to speak.

Libraries are still a place, whether it is physical or virtual. Both aspects of this hybrid home are managed by people, real live actual people with whom you will have a personal experience. You can ask the Internet a question, but how will it respond? Will it anticipate the answer with bated breath, greet data with skepticism, shush loud passers-by, or display any other famous librarian-expression? So, how does the Internet reply? Information overload.

However, data overload, the staple of the Internet, is not our enemy. It is a librarian's friend. Where data floods the senses, we provide the lifeboats. The true calling of an academic librarian is to save a scholar or a researcher the time and frustration of wafting through oceans of answers, some correct and some not.

This project is intended to help prepare future and practicing librarians to meet the challenges to our chosen profession. As we grow professionally, we gain momentum in our institution. Our libraries, however, must remain that physical/virtual hybrid: library as place, library as space. What we offer within the institution must reflect what the constituents' want, not what we think or believe they want, regardless of our conviction. Run with data, not beliefs and preconceived notions. In think, investigate, plan, and react (TIPR), my goal is to provide you with a guiding principle that provides an umbrella over which your marketing plan will grow. TIPR is your protection. It will prevent knee-jerk reactions to how we create services, resources, mission and vision statements, strategic plans, SWOT analyses, assessment tools, project plans, partnerships, and promotional methods. Use TIPR to transform the institution from a librarian-centric paradigm to its patron-centric potential.

The following chapters will guide you through discussions, examples, and instructions that you can use to create your own library marketing plans. We will learn the differences between marketing and promotions. Central to our discussion are examples and instructions you can use to create your own library marketing plan. We will also review the optimal resources and services to be promoted. These important chapters explore the twenty-first century conditions that drive the need to market not only our libraries but also our librarians, who are the true leaders and providers of twenty-first century information and literacy.

In Chapters 1 and 2, we discuss our coming to the current age. It is an organic look at the history of library marketing and promotion through the eyes of our forefathers: Drury, Dana, Ranganthan, and Green. These chapters also lay the foundation of the key principles we will discuss throughout the text: TIPR, captive audiences, librarian- and-patron centricities, marketing, promoting, and project management.

Chapter 3 dynamically presents the core of a market plan: research and assessment. We cannot react to what we have not analyzed. The profession needs to leave behind the notion that marketing is a flyer, balloon, or pencil. Marketing is not a gimmick. Marketing is research, planning, and implementing, which are three strengths we will develop herein.

In Chapter 4, we will gain a better understanding of how to use marketing tools and techniques to enhance and ultimately fulfill the mission and vision of the academic library.

In Chapter 5, we review methods by which librarians manage their marketing plan. This systematic approach streamlines the process and guides you through market plan creation and *implementation*.

Chapter 6 discusses "partnerships." As such, this enlightening chapter provides three university case reviews, compiled by evaluating the literature written about them, personal interviews conducted during onsite visits, and email exchanges. By finding other like-minded and task-oriented groups of academic library users, librarians and patrons bond.

Chapters 7 and 8 contain information on how to market and what to promote. Chapter 7 deals with what resources and services need the most exposure in the community: what to promote. We discuss current popular technological innovations and how they apply to library promotions in Chapter 8.

Chapter 9 provides a look at the twenty-first century, its challenges and opportunities, and the life of our profession and our professional spaces. It outlines methods to take our marketing plan and implementation process to understand our own opportunities by using the heretofore systematic process of marketing in the realm of librarianship.

As we move forward though these chapters, we will learn the steps in our market planning process. Enjoy the ride.

Acknowledgements

There are many individuals to whom I owe tremendous appreciation. First, I must thank my inspirational family, who tolerated my eccentric behaviors throughout the process. To Jim and Will, thank you for always bringing out the best in me. Mom, thanks for encouraging me when times get tough, for driving me across two states, and for all the laughs. It was a great experience, and one that I hold dear to my heart. I'm glad we had the chance to spend that time together. It was quite the adventure.

My deepest gratitude goes to Amy Buckley, for her keen eye to detail, and dedication to the process, as she proofed the manuscript remotely and encouraged me to do my best.

To my teachers, those who laid the foundation for my ability to craft words into knowledge, I'm indebted. Thank you to Dr. Marvin LaHood and the late Professor Charlie Adair. You taught me to think critically and to share my perspectives in a concrete and confident manner.

To Sr. Denise Roche, Dr. Arup Sen, Cheryl Saramak, and Rand Bellavia, for supporting and approving my request for a sabbatical. I am honored to be part of team that encourages scholarly creations. The experiences I was afforded, and the data I collected during my on-site visits, were amazing. To the Faculty Research team who approved my grant application, you allowed me to compile data so critical to this book. A huge thank you also goes to the Sandy Costanza for holding down the fort during my sabbatical. Thanks for your dedication to our Research and Interlibrary Loan departments. Without your work ethic, and the fact that I can depend on you implicitly, I couldn't have escaped and written this book.

Introduction

1.1 Introduction

Let's be honest: our academic libraries are at a crossroads. The decision to thrive is within our domain. It is time to begin asking ourselves tough questions. To survive is to see our library patrons enter our libraries. Thriving is a matter of understanding why they should *want* to use our libraries. Thriving is also understanding whether they find what they want when they enter the doors. It's about more than giving them what we librarians think they want. To thrive involves having them come in, teaching them to understand the resources we offer, and then continually guiding them to use the resources effectively in their scholarly pursuits. When they finally do enter the library doors, do they find what they want? Besides access to computers, do they know what to want? Or what they need to use? For the patron, it's all about what *they* want. For us to thrive, we must understand what they want. Our mission should be to form an accurate understanding of *their perceptions* of our mission in this present day of the academic library. This is the first step.

As we move into the next millennium, where our once "captive academic audience" is shifting gears and using more freely offered and simpler Internet-based tools, we race to react. However, our reactions are based on our perceptions of what we think best suits the researcher's needs and preferences. A *user-centric approach* will guide the development and the future mission of our twenty-first century libraries. This is how we must successfully compete for and win over customers who will remain loyal.

Twentieth century librarian attitudes reflected our belief that if we build it they will come. We believe students, faculty, and staff will use what we acquire. We believe that what we do for them is in their best interest. If we create new library programs and services, we believe our students will just fall in line, stumble across the newness and instantly use, appreciate, and master the resource. For example, if we build a coffee shop, our library patrons will drink coffees and teas. But do we build it in an area trafficked by students? Or are the hours adapted to their schedules? Do we incorporate access to Wi-Fi, portals, or charging stations?

Tools like Serials Solutions, Summon, and Article Linker are designed for researchers, but they really only make *our* jobs easier. And in practice it might in fact make students' jobs harder, as they try to navigate through a sea of available scholarly journal articles, popular magazine articles, print books, eBooks, and a variety of audio-visual media. A laundry list of everything they can possibly access is tantamount to a traditional google.com search. Similarly, library catalogs with tiny type fonts might be easier for the cataloging and systems librarians to administrator and design, but it will be much harder for our constituents to read, especially those in the aging population. Additionally, for students, and for skilled faculty researchers, finding the full-text article can be as difficult as finding a needle in the haystack. Admit it: if a librarian has a hard time downloading and printing a full text resource, such as an article or eBook, then the students and scholars who are working in nontraditional library spaces, such as dorm rooms, offsite computer labs, and primary residences, will give up, move on, and most likely never come back.

Our twenty-first century objective should be to recapture the attention of our audiences by focusing on a user-centric mission and vision, thus encouraging our library staff to reexamine what they do as part of the team to create an atmosphere where students thrive and succeed, while enjoying and ultimately praising our libraries. We begin with an examination of the resources and services most used by the constituents and learn as much possible about our designs, and which were created in the staff-centric mode. For example, when we discovered "discovery tools," did we decide to offer it because patrons wanted it? Did we ask them if it was in fact easier to use than our other traditional offerings, i.e., searching individual discipline-specific databases or searching each library catalog separately? In some libraries, librarians decided to purchase a discovery tool because we believed it would be easier for students to find what they need. This librarian/staff-centric approach is exactly what we need to stop doing. We need to ask questions about our potential problems before we attempt to provide solutions.

The process of creating an organizational marketing plan requires a significant level of commitment to change. It is a top-down initiative. As such, senior leaders, including directors, presidents, trustees, and others, must lead the process for the librarians and staff. Senior leaders do not need to create the plan, but they do need to support and encourage the development and implementation of the plan. They will guide the process, stepping up into expected and, indeed required, leadership roles as the marketing plan is created and subsequently implemented, and finally systematically reassessed.

As you go through the next several chapters, leave behind your current notions. Forget about what we think we know about how our constituents should be using our existing resources. If our statistics for book circulation and research desk assistance are falling, then patrons don't want what we have, need what we have, understand what we have, or, perhaps, have any idea where to begin even asking about what we have.

When we advertise our new resources and services on our library Web site, we are only focusing our attention on those clients we already have, our existing market base. Posters, pencils, and bookmarks are great and most often much appreciated, but again, we are only reaching our existing market segment base. We sometimes fail to reach outside of our comfort zone to find ways to expand our market share. Data that we obtain through user surveys and focus groups will help us better understand who uses the library, why, and why not. Understanding who *doesn't* use the library and why they don't will put us in a better position to consider and evaluate the opportunities for new programs or optimize promotions of what we do already offer. Students who use the library do so for many reasons. And if they only want to study or sleep, we still need to clearly understand who does what and why. Additionally, we need to consider our invisible market share. Why do some of our campus population not use our resources at all? Once we can answer those questions, we can begin to create a solidly successful marketing plan.

1.2 Early definitions of marketing

In 1935, the American Marketing Association (AMA) developed its first official definition of marketing, which read: "(Marketing is) the performance of business activities that direct the flow of goods and services from producers to consumers."

In our twenty-first century definition of "library marketing," we can translate the word *producers* as *librarians* and *consumers* as *library patrons*. In other words, marketing is the business of attracting library patrons to what librarians produce, our unique goods and services, which are the business activities in an academic library. The unique goods and services that exist in academic libraries traditionally include research services, book circulation, individual work spaces, group study areas, meeting spaces, and access to a variety of audio-visual equipment. Now more than ever, students need computer workstations. Other current trends include incorporating such auxiliary departments as tutoring and computer lab help desks into our existing library spaces. Additionally, some users might expect the library to provide access to new technological devices for loan (iPads, tablets, laptops, etc.) and to incorporate space for media productions and Skype-based meetings. Many libraries also incorporate more comfortable lounging areas, including both quiet areas and areas in which noise and eating are encouraged.

The definitions of marketing have changed throughout the years. In 1985, the first revisions were made to the definition. The new version read: "(Marketing is) the process of planning and executing the conception, pricing, promotion, and distribution of ideas, goods and services to create exchanges that satisfy individual and organizational objectives". In this instance, the organizational objectives in a library begin to directly relate to our mission and vision statements. As such, they guide our strategic plan, or the outline of what we say or believe we do, and will capture what we see happening in the future.

The most recently distributed definition, as agreed upon by the 2013 AMA Board of Directors, reads:

> *Marketing is the activity, set of institutions, and processes for creating, communicating, delivering, and exchanging offerings that have value for customers, partners, and society at large.*
> https://www.ama.org/AboutAMA/Pages/Definition-of-Marketing.aspx

Of the changing definition of marketing, this newest one most closely relates to the twenty-first century librarian's profession and the delivery of library resources and services. The process of creating value begins as we write the strategic plan, determine what our patrons want, give that to them, and devise communication channels where our promotional methods will be maintained and the entire process systematically reevaluated.

The biggest challenge to marketing the twenty-first century library is apprehension. Librarians are apprehensive about marketing oftentimes because they are not educated or trained in marketing principles. They believe that librarians are expected to follow the same marketing principles that for-profit organizations follow, such as the ones defined by the AMA. On the contrary, the purpose of conducting any research, whether it's a literature review, a survey, a focus group, or the collection of service-related or usage-related data is to then assemble and assimilate it. Marketing research has the same purpose. And who is better at research than librarians?

So following a business model isn't the only way to forge ahead. By developing an actual practice model for library marketing, written and developed by librarians and for use by librarians, we can move forward to a time and place where the mission of academic libraries is better understood and supported, and constituents' needs will be assessed, digested, and met.

In addition to using principles used in corporate marketing, remember to think in terms of the TIPR method: Think, Interpret, Plan, and React. In regards specifically to marketing, TIPR will help you avoid common pitfalls. For example, data generated from surveys and statistics may reflect negatively on certain departments, which might be greeted with apprehension, or even worse, hostility. In another example, data should be analyzed and discussed before being released to those it reflects. So, (T)hink first. What does this data mean and how might it be perceived by those it reflects? To interpret is to discuss your findings. What does it mean in the grander scheme of the library environment, including the image of the profession? The data will drive the discussions. When we (I)nterpret, we also begin to develop our plans of action. We talk about our opportunities. This leads us into our (P)lanning stage. How do we take the information we have and devise action plans? In other words, what do we do with the information we have. What action can we take and how is it incorporated into our marketing plan? Only after we TIP can we (R)eact. When we react, we are taking all of the information that we gathered, discussed, and analyzed so that the actions we take are based on a rational and systematic process. This is the TIPR method.

1.3 The profession: A super-marketing experience

If we agree that our constituents don't know what libraries offer, or what librarians actually do, then we agree that we cannot promote either what we do or what we offer. The mission of the academic library will falter and diminish when patrons gravitate to simpler tools that answer their questions effectively and perhaps with greater speed and ease of use, then what the library does offer. For example, Google Scholar is easier to use than Summon, as Google Scholar links to both a home library and Internet resources. These are tools that we should add to our resources, instead of shying away from its use. Google, Google Scholar, Amazon, and PubMed can easily prevent libraries and librarians from thriving. Conversely, if the librarian fails, so will the library. The existence of both will cease because inherently, one depends on the other.

Research repeatedly shows that when patrons think of libraries, the first thing that comes to mind is "books." The key activity they think librarians do is "check out books." It is not key to the survival of our profession and our libraries to be book houses or book lenders. Some librarians teach constituents how to navigate the library Web site and the World Wide Web. Others teach skills for interpreting data found on the Internet. We teach, publish, research, write, correct, order, maintain, organize, and distribute information and knowledge. However, we may falter as the gatekeepers of history and legacy while the Internet resources improve and more Web sites manage and store this data, unmitigated and free from librarian intervention.

What should we do to maintain and enhance our relevancy in the twenty-first century of high-tech innovations? Make library resources *easier* to use! We too often focus our professional preparation time on planning intricate library instruction sessions for teaching patrons to use our myriad collection, which mainly incorporates a technique to click here, or click there. We should spend that time better organizing our resources so that users no longer have to struggle to find the right place to click or to download. Again, this is inserted into a marketing plan will ensure that the librarians' goals are reachable, because the marketing plan will direct our steps and track our efforts.

The following chapters will guide you through the history of library marketing. We will also learn the differences between marketing and promotions. Central to our discussion are examples and instructions you can use to create your own library marketing plan. We will also review the optimal resources and services to be promoted. As we move forward though these chapters, we will learn the steps in our market planning process:

- Mission
- Vision
- Strategic plans
- SWOT (Strengths, Weaknesses, Opportunities, Threats)
- TIPR
- Assessment
- Project management

From the past to the future: Library as place

2

For centuries, libraries have been the cultural and historical centers of communities across the world. In medieval times, books were scarce and were too expensive to own. In a partially literate society, average citizens relied upon scholars, clergy and the privileged to interpret the written word. Before the invention of Guttenberg's printing press, libraries and scholars chained their books to lecterns and reading desks. This was done to protect the investments they had made in their book collections. By the year 1500 C.E., over 500,000 books had been produced and put into circulation. With the invention of the printing press, the written word became common in Europe. Thus mirrors the information age of the twenty-first century. The rise in reading literacy that occurred with the invention of the printing press will be followed by a rise in information literacy with the popularity and growth of the Internet and digital libraries. Librarians will take a professional step ahead, becoming the information managers of modern society. What good can services such as E-Books, Google or a Discovery Tool present, if patrons are unable to separate the wheat from the chaff, or even more simply, if they are unable to click the correct links?

The increased use of the Internet and the need for information literacy and management training can be compared to the invention of the fifteenth century printing press by Johannes Guttenberg (1398–1468 C.E.). Immediately, the printing press multiplied the number of books printed. This increased access to books for a substantial population of people who were eager to read and obtain information. After books became more readily available, reading was no longer a skill belonging only to scholars and the elite. In the seventeenth century, the daily news story developed and communicated immediate news events to mass numbers of people every day. With "Extra-Extra, Read All About It," reading became a potential skill for every man. Libraries grew as they were able to store a greater number of the monographs and serials that were being printed.

Historically, libraries have been responsible for acquiring, organizing, storing and distributing resources of all kinds. Clay tablets and scrolls may have preceded printed paper materials, but it had to be maintained and accessible at the same time. Librarianship evolved through this need to manage data and modern times have required us to now maintain electronic data, data files, data storage devices, and Internet resources. Most of the wisdom and expertise required to manage pre-Gutenberg media is still used today as we expand our data storage and retrieval role to understanding, creating, and managing open source software, open access journals, National Institutes of Health (NIH) funded studies, and Google Scholar. Google books is another resources, with such projects as Hathi Trust, that provide free Internet access to literature throughout the ages, yet maintains copyright compliance laws and regulations. E-book subscriptions currently limit interlibrary loan availability in the twenty-first century, but otherwise provide convenient access to e-content for registered and affiliated students, faculty, staff and visitors.

Marketing the 21st Century Library
© D. Lucas-Alfieri, 2015. All rights reserved.

Today's libraries must comprehensively create a modern branding and marketing campaign. They must empower themselves to explain to the constituents the limitations of our society's current search interfaces, whether they are complicated (library databases) or simplistic (Google). Through marketing and public relations campaigns, patrons better understand the role that libraries play in these pubic and academic settings.

Creating a marketing plan for libraries should be as easy as determining what and who our market base consists of, and what that market segment wants, needs, and uses. How does market planning ensure that we provide the most used and useful resources? Who decides what is used? What is useful? What does our market truly need, and what do they actually want?

Twenty-first century students need access to digital resources, from anywhere, at any time, whether it's a computer-based Web application, a book, a journal article, a required reading downloaded off a course-management site, or blogs and social media interactions and communications. These core campus activities continue to grow, evolve, and rejuvenate, at speeds librarians can maintain. We can not only exist in 50 years, but we can expand and readjust or offerings. We can still manage a library that is a place. It will still enlighten the mind. By understanding our evolutionary process, systematically market planning, we can both survive and thrive.

Attitudes of librarians have traditionally affected interest in creating marketing plans. Also to our detriment, librarians have often viewed marketing as a series of tactical events or tasks, instead of the creation of a strategic planning process. It's likened to "reactive marketing." Librarians often *start* marketing toward the actual *end* of the process, with promotions, the activities that inform our library constituents of new services, resource or events. Additionally, the tools and services are created based on what the librarians perceive their users want or need. The process is reacting to a perceived need. For example, we think students need Summon, the discovery tool that is the modern equivalent of a federated search engine, because it resembles what we think is an easy Google-search for them. So we obtain Summon and announce to our users that we now offer it. Our announcements may be in the form of flyers, pencils and balloons. The announcements are often considered to be our "marketing activities," which is merely a reaction to an event or service. In reality, we are only promoting something we think our constituents want.

In fact, librarians need to take a step backward and look toward data that will enlighten us to what our academic population actually want and need to use. Let's call this "market planning." This process involves developing one's library mission statement, and developing a sound vision of what the library will become. Collaboratively decide what services or tools should be added, deleted, improved or otherwise promoted. Remember, promoting is not market planning. Market planning involves a well thought out mission and vision statement, data gathering, managing the marketing project, and then promoting the new or existing service or resource that your patrons said they wanted or needed. Let's remember the importance here in reassessing our efforts, which then often leads to a reexamination of our collaborative efforts.

2.1 Marketing in necessity

In the profession, many mid-to-late twentieth century librarians felt their patrons were a captive audience. This was before the Internet and Google. In the twenty-first century, librarians need to begin comprehensively conducting market-based research, using surveys, comment sheets, interviews and focus groups to ascertain what patrons want. The market planning process, which will be discussed in subsequent chapters of this book, will determine the future of library services. In practice, it will be our "savior."

With increasing availability of electronic books and journal articles, easy access to online full-text via Google Scholar and HathiTrust, and constant access to the Internet, patrons can be overloaded with information options. Marketing, which again includes promotions, is a necessity. The average library user may not understand that the library has attempted to organize content on the library Web site so that it is a portal to the information they seek. If libraries can publicize such new services as instruction sessions, electronic delivery, downloads of e-books and journals, extended library hours, community service events and new library acquisitions, libraries can maintain their existence. If the librarians can better understand what their market wants, and drive changes based on that, we can determine our own destiny.

2.2 Marketing libraries in the past

Public and special libraries first marketed libraries in the late 1800s and early 1900s as our pioneering librarians espoused theories and practical tips to gain public support for the resources and services the libraries provide. Librarians across the United States understood as far back as 1865 that libraries are to be *used and useful*. Each reader should find their book. For each patron, there is a question and for each question, there is an answer.

Pioneers didn't have to contend with the Internet, and as such, their job was to attract and keep their patrons. Librarians today have to attract new patrons, retain their current patrons, and re-attract patrons who may have left the libraries for home-based Web resources. They have to convince users that libraries are as easy to use, and has the freely accessible information that the often find at home. In actuality, students have a "library in their dorm room," and professors have a library in their office, but they don't know it. We need to go a step further to provide them with a librarian in their space, not just in ours. The library Web site should be the portal to information, not Google.

"The twentieth-century library, the progressive library, would throw its doors open to all and encourage them to come in and join in the building of a community cultural center" said Renberg (1997, pp. 5–11). The sentiment can be traced back to a time before the word marketing was defined. Literature on the history of marketing United States libraries can be traced back to the late nineteenth century, when *advertising* was the key phrase of those days. Since the formal concept of marketing and developing marketing plans had yet to be defined, and since marketing encompasses so much more than flyers and newspaper articles, it was mainly advertising methods that they championed within their published articles.

2.3 Samuel Sweet Green

Samuel Sweet Green understood the importance of promoting library by promoting partnerships between librarians and their patrons. His teaching in his famously persuasive article, *Personal Relations between Librarians and Readers*, originally published in the American Library Journal in 1876, concludes that "the more freely a librarian mingles with readers, and the greater the amount of assistance he renders them, the more intense does the conviction of citizens also become, that the library is a useful institution and the more willing do they grow to grant money in larger and larger sums, to be used in buying books and employing additional assistances" (Pena & Green, 2006). Although oriented toward a public library, his sentiment holds true in academe today. Administrators and a board of directors hold the purse strings and if the primary academic customers, students and faculty, do not value the library, neither will the administrators.

Samuel Sweet Green believed that research services should be promoted to library readers so that if they have an intellectual or popular research need, they have help from what he calls a friendly and knowledgeable librarian. If librarians today continue to disseminate this theory, we can evolve into an indispensable profession of big data experts in twenty-first century society. Librarians should be viewed as the twenty-first century custodians of information. But the academic audience does not see us that way because we don't promote ourselves in a way conducive to modern library patron needs. We need proactivity.

2.4 John Cotton Dana

In 1929, John Cotton Dana said that the best publicity is word of mouth. Good service also creates a sense of esprit de corps within the library. Students will tell their classmates, faculty will tell their colleagues, and administrators will tell the board of directors that the library is full of useful books, online resources, and that it provides exceptional customer service. No matter how many resources you create to explain what an academic library does, no matter how many instructional guides are available in print or online, nothing will ever replace that human touch.

John Cotton Dana is considered to be one of the pioneering library advertisers because he convincingly discussed and encouraged librarians to advertise library resources and services, and the potential benefits to all citizens. Examples of advertising methods that he espoused included fundraising efforts, creating flyers to announce new book titles and using the mass media (namely newspapers) to list new titles or services. He said:

> If a library has or is a good thing for the community let it so be said, early, late, and often, in large, plain type. So doing shall the library's books enter—before too old to

be of service—into that state of utter worn-out-ness which is the only known bookheaven. Another way, and by some found good, is to work the sinfully indifferent first up into a library missionary, and then transform him into a patron
(Dana, 1929, p. 70)

No method is as good as positive word of mouth and good customer service. They go hand in hand. If you do a good job providing top-notch customer services such as maintaining a hold shelf, providing friendly and knowledgeable research assistance, welcoming patrons to use all library resources, giving accurate and understandable direction, having a presence in the stacks, and having a clear mission statement to follow, you will have a good image. In a Library Primer, Dana also said: "But after all, in a library as in a business, the best advertising is that done by good service. The good library is its own best advertisement." (p. 212) in about. As written in *John Cotton Dana*—http://www.ebscohost.com/resources/john-cotton-dana/about-john-cotton-dana.htm.

One of the most prestigious awards given to libraries who exemplify great public relations and education efforts is called the John Cotton Dana Award. "Dana believed … the more people knew about the library, the more they would use it. The more they used it the more they would support it and together the citizens and the library would participate in the democratic culture" as written in http://www.ebscohost.com/resources/john-cotton-dana/about-john-cotton-dana.htm.

John Cotton Dana used a multitude of resources to advertise. Among the most common, he used in-house library exhibits, newspaper articles, newsletters, pamphlets, posters, flyers and speeches to encourage library use. He urged librarians to understand the mission of their institutions from the patron's perspective (http://marketing-mantra-for-librarians.blogspot.com/2008/12/library-marketing-has-history.html).

Photos provided by the Newark Public Library.

Photos provided by the Newark Public Library.

Books in the Free Public Library

THEY belong to the citizens of Newark. The more they are used intelligently, the better for the city. If you find any of them helpful to you, if they make your hours of leisure more agreeable, your work more efficient, your enterprise more profitable and your city more enjoyable, please tell others of the fact, and thus aid in making these books more useful still.

Do what you can to prevent rough handling, mutilation and theft among these books. A few persons, unhappily, are ready to do harm to such instruments of education and progress and pleasure as our fellow citizens provide in these books.

The Free Public Library.
Newark, New Jersey.

Photos provided by the Newark Public Library.

GOOD IN ALL BOOKS

There is no booke so bad, but some commodity may be gotten by it. For as in the same pasture, the Oxe findeth fodder, the Hound a Hare; the Stork a Lizard, the faire maide flowers; so we cannot, except wee list our selves, saith Seneca, but depart the better from any booke whatsoever.

THE FREE PUBLIC LIBRARY OF NEWARK

Photos provided by the Newark Public Library.

TO NEWARK READERS

1 Reading pays.
2 Wise reading pays best.
3 Wise reading is guided reading of good things.
4 Libraries are established to collect good reading and guide in its use.
5 This Library of yours has many useful Guides and Lists and Study Courses, and Books that tell about Books on every subject,— what are the best and why. We wish these Guide Books to Reading were more used.

The Free Public Library
Newark, New Jersey

Photos provided by the Newark Public Library.

Blotter No. 1

The Beneficence of Novels

Did you ever notice how kindly you feel toward the person who has read and enjoyed the novel you have read and enjoyed? Perhaps if you read all the novels you would feel kindly toward everybody.

Try it.

Here are a few good ones:

Conqueror.	Atherton
Sea Captain.	Bailey
Clayhanger.	Bennett
Coniston.	Churchill
Woman in White.	Collins
Red Lane.	Day
Iron Woman.	Deland
Foreigner.	Gordon
Fortunate Youth.	Locke
Witness for the Defence.	Mason
Scarlet Pimpernel.	Orczy
Judgment House.	Parker
Penrod.	Tarkington
Duchess of Wrexe.	Walpole

Free Public Library, Newark, N. J.
1915

Photos provided by the Newark Public Library.

2.5 S.R. Ranganathan

In 1928, another prominent library philosopher, S.R. Ranganathan, then involved in the development of the great library at the University of Madras, wrote *The Five Laws of Library Science*. This was a period in library history when the world was grappling with fundamental questions. What is a library? What is its mission? What is library science? Libraries were just developing systems of classification and organization, and no one had yet dealt with a unified philosophy that attempted to define a simplified and universal purpose and function statement of a library. Professor Leiter comments that *The Five Laws of Library Science* "will provide us with basic tenets to guide us in performing work that fulfills our mission as keepers of the knowledge of our culture" (Leiter, 2003, p. 413).

As previously stated, medieval libraries chained books to library shelves and in doing so, limited access to cultural and intellectual information. In theory, it reduced theft and damage, thereby allowing more access to titles in their collections. However, it also limited access of books to readers, going against the teachings of Ranganathan's first rule, "books are for use." In today's twenty-first century libraries, librarians still run the risk of violating Ranganathan's first rule. Special collections, closed stacks, reserve items, off-site storage, and weeding print for electronic access are all equivalents to chaining books to library shelves. Closed stacks eliminate the ability to find books via browsing. Reserve limits circulatory use to mere hours. Off-site storage eliminates ready access, forcing patrons to decide between using interlibrary loan or a different resource entirely. Electronic resources limit access to information from the elderly and the poor, who might not have the skills or resources to use computers and electronic resources, both within and outside of the library. "A library must formulate policies that ensure that the collection it is building and maintaining is adequate to fulfill the expectations of its community of users. In other words, the collection must be appropriate to the library's mission," (Leiter, p. 415). The libraries' mission, after all, defines what is done, and is the basis for all library market planning.

2.6 Francis K.W. Drury

Finding literature on this history of marketing academic libraries is difficult, as scant evidence of a systematic development of a philosophical or structured implementation of marketing plans in academics can be found. In other words, market planning pioneers were public librarians, not academic librarians. In fact, our early American academic library staff were campus teaching faculty or professors, not trained specifically as professional librarians.

Perhaps the earliest article on marketing college libraries could be Francis K.W. Drury's piece called "*Publicity for College Libraries*," published in The Library Journal in 1920. He wrote that our commodities in 1920 included services such as reference and general reading resources and materials. He also stated that the library provides customer service and research assistance at circulation and research desks, and through resource lists, instructional documents, indexes, and a general schematic for the organization of information.

His early wisdom resonates today, as these are the same resources and services provided by the twenty-first century library. Today, we also offer some services he does not list, such as access to computers for Internet surfing, word processing and other specialized software, such as SPSS statistical software, typing tests, and Moodle or Blackboard course implementation software. Computer usage in some ways may be our most popular and most heavily used service. It is undeniably the most heavily used commodity in the library. Modern academic libraries have also made strides to consolidate a multitude of campus resources. Sometimes they relinquish shelf space to tutoring staff, computer technology support staff, and writing resource assistance. Other times, libraries may actually expand their footprint to add these same campus resources.

He wrote that we need to advertise. The first step was to catch their attention, which was difficult, he said. "Will students notice anything these days unless it is hung from balloons or bannered across the street?" he said (p. 488). He also selects the main methods or types of advertising, the classified, "Wanted, 300 freshman to use the library every week," (p. 488), with the publicity, advertisements, billboards, street banners and bulletin boards. He said to display advertisements and create promotions in:

- Newspapers, magazines, periodicals and trade papers.
- Circulars and handbills.
- Novelties such as calendars, bookmarks, and pencils.
- Registers, directories and theater programs.
- Delivery wagons, street banners and floats.
- Samples, catalogs, agents and traveling men.
- And through courteous service.

2.7 Early academic marketing steps

In the late 1800s, as graduate programs were introduced, academic libraries became a prominent feature of college campuses as academic libraries grew even further in size and prominence. The increased prominence mandated a new level of instruction, so that library patrons better understood what libraries offered. Bibliographic instruction became a tool by which library services were announced and thereby promoted. Early professors and academic librarians lectured, gave orientation tours, and organized reader advisories and book talks, in ways similar public librarian efforts at that time.

Creating reader's advisories were one of the earliest promotional activities of academic librarians assumed, in the name of promoting its resources. According to Janelle Zauha, in the 1920s and 1930s there was a push for academic librarians to promote reading. "For example, by 1939, there were no less than four recreational reading collections located throughout the University of Iowa campus in 'browsing' libraries" (Zauha, 1993, p. 57).

In his article, *College Libraries as Aids to Instruction*, Professor Justin Winsor said "we have not discovered what the full functions of college library should be…we have not organized that instruction which teaches how to work its collections as place or treasures," (1920, p. 7). Early marketing efforts in academic libraries are seen as imbedded accidentally in library bibliographic instruction. The librarian has to campaign and force ranks into action, he said.

And bibliographic instruction was born. "It would be a good plan to take the students by sections, and make them acquainted with the bibliographic apparatus, those books that the librarian finds his necessary companions, telling the peculiar value of each, how his assists in such cases, that in others; how this may lead to that, until with practice the students finds that for his work he has almost a new sense." (Winsor, 1920, p. 9).

2.8 The future

All of these changes must be affectively marketed. Twentieth century librarians considered their patrons base to be a captive audience because there was no such competition as the Internet or Google. Future libraries conduct market-based research, using surveys, comment sheets, interviews and focus groups to ascertain what patrons want. The marketing and research determine the future of library services.

With increasing availability of electronic information, access to Google Scholar, publishers self-indexing and e-books, many library patrons feel overloaded with information options. Publicizing such new services as instruction sessions, electronic delivery, downloads of e-books and journals, extended library hours, community service events and new library acquisitions help libraries drive their own futures.

Conceptually, librarians can follow in the footsteps of our founding fathers, Dana, Ranganathan, Green, Drury, and Windsor, who each instilled a level of eminence in our mission to let the communities we serve better understand what we offer to them. A library does not exist for the use of librarians, it is for the people. It should also be *by the people*.

Some changes will seem to be mandated, i.e., we don't decide to make the technological changes that are "thrust" upon us. But these technological changes will dictate the future, and librarians need to become more integral in the changes in technology related to library services.

Today, popular Google results contain Web site content created by general members of society intended to be read by general members of society. Examples of such include commercial sites for shopping, current events or happenings in a specific region, general blogs and opinion pieces. Technical Google research results may consist of materials written for people belonging to medical, scientific or academic institutions. Scholarly Google results appear because Google aligned itself with publishers and indexed journal content. Now, Google Scholar in many cases replaces a researcher's need to use library databases. It presents citation results from the publisher's journals, including specialized scholarly articles, popular magazines and newspapers. However, scholarly information, popular literature and archived newspaper content are not readily available in a full-text format through Google Scholar. Libraries continue to take the lead in providing the free full-text that Google cannot.

In academe, this interaction must be a seamless transaction. Instead of using a teacher–student model in which library patrons are taught to search library holding independently, academic and school librarians provide the full-text research material with no questions asked or instructions provided. Such a model will more closely follow services provided in law firms or hospitals, where users' needs are met with full-service transactions.

The printed book will not be replaced by electronic copies until the mid-to-late twenty-first century, as e-books become more readily available and compliant with copyright laws. Future technology begins to provide better reader interfaces. E-book readers such as digital books by Sony Reader and the Kindle have not yet progressed to the level of sophistication that readers prefer. The future e-book readers become an electronic projection, mirroring a movie or television screen that is touch activated. Users can flip pages with their fingertips. E-book readers become like staples in every local public and academic library. The future Google replaces traditional library on-line catalogs and databases. New social user interfaces develop, so that library patrons and the general public can tag keywords, rank items, and suggest similar resources that would be found in catalogs and databases.

Single federated search engines streamline the research process. As people become more accustomed to the single research Google interface, libraries adapt. Today's patrons need to first know if they want a book, videocassette, DVD, a reference resource, or a journal article. Second, patrons must select the proper search tool, be it an online database, library catalog, or in the library's print collection. Futuristic models, already being incorporated in the library world by such services as 360 Search, Search It and Credo Reference, allow patrons to search key word terms in one search box, with results immediately appearing from a multitude of resources, including books, journal articles, encyclopedias and Web sites. This is the way of the future library.

We must understand that in the near future, technology will drive us forward. We are driven also by our customer needs and desires. We need to capture the reigns. What do they say they want and need? We must move forward prepared to meet technology head on, promoting and educating our patrons along the way. To promote is to educate and we are inherently good at that.

2.9 Librarians of the future offer full-text delivery seamlessly

There are many constituents who comprise our core group of library customers. Namely, we have students and faculty, our heaviest user groups. Each constituency has unique library needs. Students, our largest population of users, need computers, work spaces, study spaces, presentation preparation spaces, books, journal articles, archives, etc. Faculty might need course review materials, books and journal articles. The students and the faculty are our primary customer. We should center our efforts on them. To serve their needs is the most primary reason for our existence.

However, we also have a core group of additional users who cannot be overlooked. We have officers and trustees, administrators, overall college and community members, alumni, and other colleges and universities. Trustees and board members might need to access archives or official records of the college. Alumni and general community or special visitors are interested in using computers and retrieving journal articles, books, or even to spend time playing video games or using social media. Our relationship with other colleges and universities might involve our reciprocal agreements, such as with ILL or in-person book check-outs.

Also, the people, our constituents, should dictate our future paths. Think: what is it they want, not what is it we think they should want. Think: what do they need to use, not what do we want them to use. Market planning begins with an assessment of all we can do.

The same events are unfolding in the electronic information age. In the immediate future, libraries house more computers and less books in the Guttenberg print format. Information literacy increases in a way similar to how the Guttenberg printing press increased reading literacy. Instead of relying solely on the use of larger desktop PC models, future libraries will begin to lend out cell phones, e-book readers, and other handheld devices. As the move to an online and virtually connected world increases, the general populations of today need to learn an entirely new skill set. Public libraries can collaborate with primary and secondary school educators, especially in economically disadvantaged neighborhoods, to increase information and technology literacy.

In future libraries, an increased need for electronic tutorials develops. Traditionally, librarians now hold in-person instruction sessions in a lecture-based or active learning model. That becomes less common as electronic tutorials become more readily available. Students become more interested in learning how to use the library and they want to learn this via online Web-based tutorials. Students and other library patrons can access these tutorials anywhere that they have an Internet connection.

The following chapters will guide you through the processes and the methods that can devise your plan for promoting the library of the future, the one you create through analysis, design, and promotion.

2.10 Conclusion

The charge to begin advertising libraries began late in the 1800s and in many ways, it continues today. Early efforts of library pioneers exemplify that it has always been important to bring to light the resources and services libraries provide not only to the general public, but to college students, academics, scholars, and other primary library constituencies.

The roots of academic library advertising begin with reader's advisory groups, library instruction, and orientation sessions.

2.11 Discussion questions

1. List three of the earliest advertising/promotional methods that were encouraged by John Cotton Dana and Samuel Sweet Green.
2. What services do twenty-first century libraries offer that were not offered in the late 1800s?

3. Library advertising was first discussed and encouraged by public librarians as early as the late 1800s. Discuss reasons that were valid for that time for public librarians led the charge, instead of academics.
4. What role did bibliographic instruction play in the development of library advertising?

References

Dana, J. C. (1929). *A library primer*. Chicago: Library Bureau.

Drury, F. K. W. (1920). Publicity for college libraries. *Library Journal, 45*, 487–489.

Gupta, D. K. (2008). *Library marketing has a history*. Retrieved from, http://marketing-mantra-for-librarians.blogspot.com/2008/12/library-marketing-has-history.html.

Leiter, R. A. (2003). Reflections on Ranganathan's five laws. *Law Library Journal, 95*(3), 411–418.

Pena, D., & Green, S. S. (2006). Personal relations between librarians and readers. *Journal of Access Services, 4*(1–2), 157–167. Reprinted from *Library Journal*, 1, 74–81 (1876).

Ranganathan, S. R. (1931). *The five laws of library science*. London: Edward Goldston, Ltd.

Renberg, G. (1997). Marketing library services: How it all began. In R. Savard (Ed.), *Adapting marketing to libraries in a changing world wide environment*. Papers presented at the 63rd IFLA Conference, Copenhagen, September 1997.

Winsor, J. (1920). *College libraries as aids to instruction*. Washington: GPO.

Zauha, J. M. (1993). Recreational reading in academic browsing rooms: Resources for readers' advisory. *Collection Building, 12*(3/4), 57–62.

Marketing plan research and assessment   3

As we progress through the steps required to create library marketing plans, it's essential to understand the terms commonly used in modern research. The following definitions are taken from the *APA Dictionary of Statistics and Research Methods;* Sheldon Zedeck (2013).

Action research—"socially useful and theoretically meaningful research developed and carried out in response to a social issue or problem, results of which are applied to improve the situation (e.g. by changing existing or developing new public policies)" (pp. 3–4).

Applied research—"studies conducted to solve real-world problems, as opposed to studies that are carried out to develop a theory or to extend basic knowledge" (p. 12).

Case study—"an in-depth investigation of a single individual, family, event, or other entity. Multiple types of data (psychological, physiological, biographical, environmental) are assembled, for example, to understand an individual's background, relationship, and behavior. Although case studies allow for intense analysis of an issue, they are limited in the extent to which their findings might be generalized" (p. 37).

Empirical method—"a procedure for conducting an investigation that relies upon experimentation and systematic observation rather than theoretical speculation. The term is sometimes used as a vague synonym for the *scientific method*" (p. 112).

Focus group—"a small set of people, typically 8–12 in number, who share common characteristics (e.g., working parents with 5-to-8 year old children) that are relevant to the research question and who are selected to discuss a topic of which they have personal experience (e.g., their children's reading abilities and school performance). A leader conducts the discussion and keeps it on target while also encouraging free-flowing, open-ended debate. Originally used in marketing to determine consumer response to particular products, focus groups are now used to determining typical reactions, adaptations and solutions to any number of issues, events, or topics, and are associated particularly with QUALITATIVE RESEARCH" (p. 140).

Hypothesis—"an empirical testable proposition about some fact, behavior, relationship, or the like, usually based on theory, that states an expected outcome resulting from specific conditions or assumptions" (p. 169).

Institutional Review Board (IRB)—"a committee named by an agency or institution to review research proposals originating within that agency for ethical acceptability and compliance with the organization's codes of conduct. IRBs help protect research participants and are mandatory at any U.S. institution receiving federal funds for research" (p. 176).

Interviews—"a directed conversation in which a researcher, therapist, clinician, employer, or the like (the interviewer) intends to elicit specific information from an individual (the interviewee) for purposes of research, diagnosis, treatment, or employment. Conducted face to face or by telephone, interviews may be either standardized, including set questions, or open ended, varying with material introduced in responses by the interviewee. Their RELIABILITY is of particular concern, and interviewers must be careful to minimize or eliminate personal judgment and biases in evaluating responses" (p. 181).

Meta-analysis—"a quantitative technique for synthesizing the results of multiple studies of a phenomenon into a single result by combining the effect size estimates from each study into a single estimate of the combined effect size or into a distribution of effect sizes" (p. 213).

Qualitative research—"a method of research that produces descriptive (non-numerical) data, such as observations of behavior or personal accounts of experiences. The goal of gathering this qualitative data is to examine how individuals can perceive the world from different vantage points. A variety of techniques are subsumed under qualitative research, including content analysis of narratives, in-depth interviews, focus groups, participant observation, and case studies, often conducted in naturalistic settings. Also called qualitative design; qualitative inquiry, qualitative method; qualitative study. Compare QUANTITATIVE RESEARCH" (p. 282).

Quantitative research—"a method of research that relies on measuring variables using a numerical system, analyzing these measurements using any of a variety of statistical models, and reporting relationships and associations and associations among the studied variables. For example these variables may be test scores for measurements of reaction time. The goal of gathering this quantitative data is to understand, describe, and predict the nature of a phenomenon, particularly through the development of models and theories. Quantitative research techniques include experiments and surveys. Also called quantitative design; quantitative inquiry; quantitative methods; quantitative study. Compare QUALITATIVE RESEARCH" (pp. 284–285).

Research method—"a procedure for the formulation and evaluation of hypotheses that is intended to reveal relationships between variables and provide an understanding of the phenomenon under investigation. In psychology, this generally involves EMPIRICAL TESTING and takes the form of the scientific method. See also QUALITATIVE RESEARCH; QUANTITATIVE RESEARCH" (p. 311).

Reliability—"the trustworthiness or consistency of a measure, that is, the degree to which a test or other measurement instrument is free of random error, yielding the same results across multiple applications to the same sample" (p. 307).

Survey—"a study in which a group of participants is selected from a population and some selected data about or opinion of those participants are collected, measured, and analyzed. Information typically is gathered by interview or self-report questionnaire, and the results thus obtained may then be extrapolated to the whole population" (p. 365).

Statistical significance—"the degree to which a research outcome cannot reasonably be attributed to the operation of chance or random factors…significance generally is a function of sample size—the larger the sample, the less likely it is that one's findings will have occurred by chance" (p. 355).

Systematic review—"an organized method of locating, assembling, and evaluating a body of literature on a particular topic using a specific set of criteria" (p. 369).

Validity—"the degree to which empirical evidence and theoretical rationales support the adequacy and appropriateness of conclusions drawn from some form of assessment" (p. 404).

3.1 Using quantitative and qualitative data

Quantitative research methods include a structured approach to gathering data. This can be a problem-solving approach, quantifying concepts so problems can be evaluated, discussed and resolved. When librarians gather quantitative data, it is so they can understand and anticipate something they have yet to define or that which alludes them. For example, librarians are unsure why reference desk transactions are slipping. To prevent the knee-jerk reaction of deciding to promote or change existing services, librarians should first review the literature and then create surveys that gather quantitative data. Quantitative data is most often expressed in numbers or statistical correlates.

Qualitative research methods focus on observing patron behaviors, attitudes and opinions so that we can understand why they behave the way they do, and to discover what they want us to deliver. This information is presented in anecdotal terms, unlike quantitative research, which presents findings numerically. Often, qualitative data can be massaged into a series of themes. For example, librarians involved in the research process can devise a series of focus groups designed to gather data about why students are not using the research desk. In one case study, suppose that librarians found some professors told their students to use a local university library instead of the campus library. The university, they said, has more resources. In this example, perhaps the faculty need in-servicing to better understand what the home campus library actually subscribes to for meeting their students' needs. This would in effect increase the number of reference transactions when students need assistance using the home library.

Some research takes the form of both quantitative and qualitative methods, perhaps by coupling a series of Likert scale questions with open-ended comment questions in the survey assessment. Some surveys may include both types of questions to ease the burden to the survey pool; often, students are busy with their coursework and might skip participating altogether, making it wise to keep the survey short and include both quantitative and qualitative questions. Additionally, when assessing user services to determine whether the library's services are unique, easy to use, easy to find, or convenient to use, we should locate the most appropriate user base: those who are most likely to participate, such as "library friends" or frequent users. Student workers are also helpful participants when the time comes to gather data. Also, when evaluating program or service satisfaction, locate a survey pool of experienced users, not a survey pool of the entire campus. If the end result is to improve ILL services to the community, ask current users what works and what can be improved. The general campus will not know the answers to any intimate ILL questions and their responses can skew the results. Similarly, a survey to assess knowledge or awareness of the ILL program in general can be sent to the entire campus, and it can simultaneously help promote the service.

Use both qualitative and quantitative data to produce the most robust results possible, which will ultimately identify opportunities for improvement. For example, administer a survey (quantitative) and conduct focus group sessions (qualitative), to glean good data based on real-life customer perceptions and experiences.

Use the think, vestigate, plan, react (TIPR) method to launch this research and assessment phase. When thinking about the problem or the data needed, start with a literature review. Then interpret via tailored qualitative and quantitative research studies. Planning indicates the progress of a marketing plan from its development to implementation, and reacting involves the actual service improvements, creations and promotions entailed in that marketing plan. Leslie Farmer supports this process. She explains (2011, p. 5) that theoretically, research is an extension of problem solving in which librarians:

- Identify a problem
- Identify significant factors, brain storm possible solutions
- Determine possible consequences, choose and implement one solution
- And evaluate its effectiveness.

Think how TIPR will improve the overall marketing plan. Farmer says that research is a systematic process by which we investigate a topic and its context by "strategically gathering data and analyzing them and then sharing the findings and recommendations. The strategy or method used needs to be valid, measuring the intended factor, and [whether it is] reliable, that is, capable of being replicated with the same results" (p. 6).

3.2 Using action research

A very common research method is called action research. It is a systematic method used to examine the work environment, deconstruct problems, and gather data. Action research also includes analyzing the data, developing actionable conclusions, and writing recommendations. In many ways, it was both participatory and practical when it was first developed by sociologists in the 1940s. Since then, it has evolved to a localized and quasi-experimental research method, a way to systematically approach and investigate what makes people find what works, and what effective solutions they can employ. According to Farmer, it involves examining one's services and practices so that they can be improved. A cycle of inquiry develops as data are generated and questions emerge, she says.

From here can be drawn theories and general conclusions. "Identify a number of qualitative studies of similar phenomena," says Farmer (p. 6). She suggests we take into account "varying settings or demographics of the participating populations, the researcher can (then) build a case that holds for many situations" (p. 6). She calls this research meta-analysis, and since the data arises from natural settings, they can still reflect qualitative perspectives. Action research, according to Farmer, is when we systematically examine the work environment, define its problems, gather data about it, analyze it, draw conclusions and then act on it. This protocol is mirrored in the TIPR method.

Marie Radford concurs, "It has become essential for librarians to respond appropriately by conducting, analyzing, and implementing the results of empirical investigations designed to determine the right mode and mix of services, programs, and resources (print and online) for their specific user communities" (2011, p. xi). Radford also distinguishes between the types and value of data that can be collected: "statistical and quantitative methods are of ongoing importance, but frequently these numerical results can be difficult to interpret. For example how specifically can services be improved when people have consistently related library service as *Excellent* when asked by quantitative surveys?" In her scholarly work, she's attracted to qualitative data to better explore and unravel the complexities of human interaction with the library. "The professional literature shows that many research studies have embraced these approaches, yet lack of training and, perhaps, the perceived subjective nature of these methods have continued to be barriers for library practitioners" (p. xii).

Radford says, "For example, a Web-based survey using Survey Monkey, Zoomerang, or a comparable product can be inexpensive, and results are quickly obtained, with tables of numerical data ready to be cut and pasted into a report. However, a few open-ended, qualitative questions added to the survey can be extremely helpful in contextualizing the results and in producing illustrative and often telling quotations in the respondent's voice." She further suggests that action research initiatives be undertaken by professions who are responsible for creating strategic plans in individual departments, service areas, or the library as a whole.

One of the most practical methods for library research is a mixed approach, where both qualitative and quantitative data are gathered and assessed. Alone, quantitative data, or data driven by numbers, will not provide a complete picture. When distributed and collected without qualitative data, quantifiable information lacks depth. Generally, a more subjective analysis of the situation in question, for example via focus groups, interviews, and observations, is needed to glean a complete picture of the challenge ahead. It is imperative to gather as complete a picture as possible to truly understand what opportunity for improvement actually exists. Assessment of the best data available must be conducted as part of creating the marketing plan. It is this discovery period, or investigation, via which the twenty-first century librarian seeks out questions and answers regarding the library's opportunities for improvement.

3.3 Assessment tools

Assessment tools can be used to gather the data needed to drive the library's marketing plan forward, and provide the team with intellectual resources needed to create initiatives. The data will outline opportunities for improvements within the library. The most commonly used data collection tools employed by adapting libraries are the questionnaire survey, the focus group interview and the personal interview. Some researchers find great success in using two or more research tools, for example a questionnaire followed by focus groups or interviews.

3.3.1 Questionnaire survey

Again, the TIPR method is employed in creating, distributing, and effectively implementing actions according to the team's findings. According to Powell and Connaway, the academic library's planning *process* is key to success (2004). Some steps they consider helpful, which mirror TIPR (in a process Powell and Connaway call Think and Investigate), are listed below.

- Define the problem
- Review other research (literature reviews)
- Hypothesize solutions

- Identify information needed to hypothesize. Plan the data presentation and analysis
- Identify potential respondents or subjects
- Select the most appropriate technique for collecting data

Questionnaire surveys that are completed anonymously often offer frank and honest, and therefore, the most beneficial data. As such, these tools can reduce administrator biases. Such biases can include leading answers, or rephrasing questions such that the meanings change. According to Powell and Connaway, this type of survey eliminates variation in the questioning process. The content and the organization of the questions remains constant, they say.

As another benefit, questionnaire surveys allow participants time to complete the surveys at their leisure. Quantitative data and qualitative data can both be gleaned. However, these surveys can range from being very inexpensive (SurveyMonkey) to very expensive (LibQual).

SurveyMonkey has 15 question types, including rating scales and multiple choice. It's possible to create online surveys from scratch, or choose questions from Question Bank, SurveyMonkey's collection of question templates. Using one URL, the survey process may include links on emails, Web sites, Twitter, Facebook, and more. For more information, see https://www.surveymonkey.com/mp/take-a-tour/?ut_source=header.

LibQual is a survey tool designed specifically for libraries. According to the LibQual Web site:

> LibQual+ is a suite of services that libraries use to solicit, track, understand, and act upon users' opinions of service quality. These services are offered to the library community by the Association of Research Libraries (ARL). The program's centerpiece is a rigorously tested Web-based survey bundled with training that helps libraries assess and improve library services, change organizational culture, and market the library. http://www.libqual.org/about/about_lq/general_info

The goals of LibQUAL+ are to:

- Foster a culture of excellence in providing library service
- Help libraries better understand user perceptions of library service quality
- Collect and interpret library user feedback systematically over time
- Provide libraries with comparable assessment information from peer institutions
- Identify best practices in library service
- Enhance library staff members' analytical skills for interpreting and acting on data

If the library is on a budget or has a small staff, SurveyMonkey may be a cost-effective, easy-to-use method for preparing an effective survey tool. Libraries with limited resources may also employ the assistance of an intern, student, campus staff or professor in the field of survey methods or marketing to assist with survey creation and implementation. Some skilled people may be willing to volunteer or accept a small honorarium for their services.

The questionnaires must be pretested. During pretesting, a sample size of participants will test the survey and provide feedback as to whether the survey is confusing or difficult to complete. Such a pretest also allows the creator the opportunity to ask questions of the test participants, to ensure that the survey is the best tool possible. This must be done before the survey final edits are completed.

Be aware that creating the shortest survey tool will help librarians gather the best and most complete data as possible. According Powell and Connaway, "there are a variety of steps one can take to keep the questionnaire length to a minimum" (p. 41). They suggest the following:

- Keep the instructions clear and brief.
- When mailing surveys, print on both sides of the paper.
- Only ask for information that the researcher does not already have.

Powell and Connaway agree that survey respondents should be screened so that they are not answering the questions that do not apply to them. As previously discussed, if the purpose is to a assess patron perceptions of the library's Interlibrary Loan program, only send surveys, whether Web links or paper surveys, to ILL users; screen out non-users. Remember also that all surveys, whether paper or electronic, need a brief introductory cover letter, one that describes the content of the survey, the survey's purpose and how the data and results will be distributed. It is important to also at this point assure anonymity. Obviously, researchers will distribute paper surveys by mail, or by placing them around well trafficked areas in the library or campus. Distribute electronic surveys by emailing Web links, or, if appropriate, post Web links on the library Web site, Facebook, Twitter; it is also possible to hand out paper slips or book marks with a URL to follow. Remember to include a cover letter, or, if space is limited, a catchy brief description instead. Send out postcard reminders, in either print or electronic form, to remind participants when the survey is due.

Extend the date if necessary to achieve an optimal response rate. The response rate is the number of surveys returned divided by the number of surveys distributed. Statistical significance is related to response rate because researchers want the results to reflect reality. The higher the response rate, the more statistically significant because the results are less likely to be the result of chance. Research shows that response rates are higher for print surveys compared to electronically distributed surveys. According to Sauermann and Roach, "more detailed online surveys often exhibit lower response rates of around 10–25%. Low response rates, in turn, reduce sample size and statistical power. Moreover, low response rates may also lead to nonresponsive bias and affect the validity of survey results irrespective of the sample size" (2013, p. 273).

3.3.2 Focus group or personal interview?

Focus groups and personal interviews are the most common ways to obtain actionable qualitative data. Why chose one over the other? Both are beneficial and both have their own unique qualities. Table 3.1 outlines the similarities and differences.

Focus groups are a means to convene a forum for discussing and compiling new ideas. It is important to have skilled and experienced moderators who are objective. Often, survey participants are selected to participate in the group discussions, and are given a follow up survey in addition.

In a focus group setting, the moderator maintains control of the discussion and ensures that participants' conversation doesn't stray too far off the topic on hand. The moderator concentrates more on the flow of the discussion rather than on the details

Table 3.1 **Similarities and differences between focus groups and personal interviews**

Focus groups	Personal interviews
Convenes a forum of participants and conducts research in a group	Convenes participants and conducts research individually
Participants may be interrupted by the comments of others	Each participant fully describes their experiences or opinions
Participants' ideas help form themes organically	Participants comment individually so themes must be compiled
Conversations stream based on group comments	Conversations are directed by the interviewer's questions and follow ups
Conversations may stray off track	Conversation stays on track

or individual responses. Valentine says that using focus groups helps themes emerge naturally as students respond to one another's comments. As one benefit, focus groups reach more participants in a shorter period of time, compared to the time it would take to interview each student individually.

The individual interviews offer in many aspects the exact opposite data-gathering experience. Advantages of interviews include giving each student the opportunity to fully describe experiences, without interruptions such as those often seen in focus groups (Valentine, 1993, p. 310). Interviewers have a unique ability to influence the direction of any conversation in individual interviews. Valentine recalls an instance in which student interview subjects wanted assurances that they were providing correct answers. Additionally, while focus groups run themselves with conversational steam, the interview is managed solely by the interviewer. Both methods can be used to gather unique and useful data.

For example, at the Linfield College library, Valentine used qualitative methods for an assessment, explaining that her study was designed to "circumvent professional wisdom and find a theory of behavior based on what students themselves think" (p. 300). She believes that the qualitative approach to data helps to develop theories based on ordinary every-day experiences.

In her study, she used both focus groups and individual interviews, two qualitative assessment tools designed to gather opinions and personal narratives regarding the information-seeking behaviors of the students at Linfield College. Additionally, it is possible to use the same questions for both data-gathering methods.

Focus groups can provide exceptional marketing data when they precede paper and electronic survey assessments. In other words, qualitative assessments should follow quantitative data. The data from the survey can be extrapolated and massaged to help form the focus group or interview questions. With focus groups, the quantitative results will form the script given the moderator. The moderator may be a librarian, but many library experts recommend selecting a marketing and opinion research professional (Shoaf, 2003, p. 130). These experts can solicit responses to the scripted questions without influencing the results. For example, if the focus group moderator is a librarian participants recognize or know on a professional level, participants may not react in absolutely honest terms. In other words, they might hold back criticism or other worthwhile information. That will skew results. "The danger to valid results is that responses can be skewed by the social interaction between MR (marketing researcher) and group, and by the group dynamics of the participants" (Shoaf, 2003, p. 130). When MRs announce that they have no affiliation with the library, they will put the participants at ease with the process of disclosure.

Focus group data may cause hurt feelings among the staff, especially when the criticism is harsh, or when people feel singled out by the comments. It is important to encourage the staff to look at the data objectively, and to help them understand that the data will provide many opportunities for positive changes and improvements.

Personal interviews are similar to focus groups because they are created as a question/answer interaction. Interviews can be video or audio recorded and then transcribed. As with questionnaires and focus groups, interviews can be pretested using a small sample of staff or "friends" of the library. Use the same or slightly varied focus group questions in personal interviews as well so that the resultant data comments and themes can be compared to those gathered via focus group sessions.

Powell and Connaway stress the importance of interviewer objectivity and emphasize that care should be taken not to lead responses. "In obtaining or encouraging responses, the interviewer may find it necessary to repeat certain questions" (p. 148). However, they warn interviewers against significantly changing the wording of the question, as it might solicit inaccurate responses. For clarification, they say, ask interviewees to elaborate on responses. Avoid interviewer biases, a leading disadvantage of interviews. Perhaps the most important benefit of using the personal interview is that it generates a higher response rate.

Internet interviews diminish the chance of biases. According to Powell and Connaway, "the internet interview utilizes computer-mediated communication (CMC) which allows humans to interact directly with each other in synchronous or real time using monitors texts and keyboards" (p. 149). However, they point out that it is more difficult to establish a good rapport online than in person.

In our approach to this big picture, we first gather data in the form of comments, surveys, ratings, and suggestions for improvement.

To improve quality, we must improve customer service. It is a continual process. We must first assess our current customer service, by conducting surveys, running focus groups, and creating a team to analyze the data. We can use the same process employed in investigating the effectiveness and challenges of the library.

We must obtain a commitment to improve customer service from the entire library staff, not just those on the marketing team. Without this organizational commitment, the efforts of the team will be fruitless.

After gathering and analyzing the data, we need to set and define clear objectives. Do not use generalities:

YES
Increase circulation of academic DVD titles to faculty by 10% over the next two semesters.

NO
Increase circulation of library materials to faculty.

In defining our roles within the modern academic institution, we must keep open lines of communication, from the top of the management structure down to the lower level support staff.

We must strive to avoid creating library-centric service, policy or procedure improvements. Efforts should all keep the patron in mind: user-centric.

Why are we worried? Even premier research universities question the future of libraries, and hence the survival of librarians nationwide.

3.4 Avoiding assessment challenges

As the marketing plan begins to unfold, and action has been taken regarding the services or resources the library team has decided to offer, the team will need to assess the results of change. This reassessment phase is ongoing, and will provide meaningful comparative data, as long as the assessment tools are designed to measure "apples to apples." Research design and data interpretation go hand in hand, providing a complete picture of your immediate organization and the proposed future of the organization, as the marketing plan proceeds to be implemented.

- Be careful of *how* and *when* questions are asked. Begin on a positive note, asking perhaps about the respondent's level of satisfaction with a popular service or resource. Asking a negative question first will give respondents a negative outlook and may skew results.
- Incorporate both close-ended and open-ended questions. *Include* a comment section or a "please explain" section to solicit additional information on a particular matter. This provides participants with a chance to give ideas or list circumstances that the survey writer overlooked or hadn't considered.
- Be wary of using the most convenient survey pool. This will only generate convenient data. In the example discussed before, an initial survey for an interlibrary loan service, only users of the service are surveyed, pulling email addresses from their user accounts. This entails what might equate to hours of data generation to find the appropriate clients to gage their satisfaction and recommendations for this program. To gather good data to drive improvements in existing programs and services, simply sending out a blast email to the entire college community will not work. Members of the college community as a whole may not use the service, or even be aware of the service, so they are certainly not aware of what works well, or what improvements the service might need. Including this population in the survey will result in skewed data. Moreover, when reassessing the ILL service, the survey administrators must use a similarly selected survey pool each time (that is, users of the service) in order to compare "apples to apples."
- Another challenge to data collection is gathering only information the team wants to find. Be aware that the team might think an issue exists that truly does not. Authors in "Practical Research Methods for Librarians and Information Professionals" (Beck and Manuel, 2008) say that it is difficult for researchers to separate what they see, from that they expect to see, from what they want to find. Also be wary of jumping to conclusions. The data must be significant and reliable. Questions can be followed up using comments (such as an interview) so that researchers are not concluding anything untrue based on their own preconceived notions. For example, a library may want to assess research desk usage because the number of research questions asked has declined over the last 3 years. Some librarians are convinced that it is because the college community is unaware that the service exists, or that students

don't understand what the librarian stations are there for. In reality, for this example, students commented that the librarians always looked too busy to assist, even when they weren't assisting other patrons. The data gathered should lead the library team to an understanding of the best improvement plans possible, the library's best data is what will be incorporates into the marketing plans. The better the data, the better the plan.

3.5 IRB process

Finally, it is good to keep in mind the Code of Federal Regulations, Section 46 of Title 45, in which the institutional review board (IRB) is described as a check and balance to the research process. The IRB process involves an official notification of the intent, normally involving documentation of the process and the intent. An internal IRB reviews and then approves the application. The IRB is designed to ensure that "all research involving human subjects conducted, supported, or otherwise subject to regulation by any Federal Department or Agency" is compliant to the following seven criteria (Beck and Manuel, 2008, p. 255):

1. Risks to subjects are minimized
2. Risks to subjects are reasonable in relation to the anticipated benefits
3. Selection of subjects is equitable
4. Informed consent is obtained from each subject or their legal representative
5. Informed consent is appropriately documented
6. The research plan makes provisions for monitoring data collection to ensure safety for subjects
7. Adequate provisions are made to protect the privacy of all participants

3.6 Conclusion

Investigate the status of a library's services and resources, plus discover what the library's constituents actually want by gathering good data. First, conduct literature reviews. What do previously collected data show? Then conduct a carefully considered series of surveys, focus groups and interviews. The surveys will uncover statistics and themes. Conduct focus groups as needed to expand on the statistics and themes gathered. Personal interviews again can expound on the survey data. All combined, this meets the Interpretative phase of the TIPRMethod.

3.7 Review questions

1. What is the difference between quantitative and qualitative research?
2. Explain why researchers might choose to conduct a questionnaire survey before a focus group.
3. What is a focus group moderator? Who might best fill this position?
4. Define response rate and statistical significance.

References

Beck, S. E., & Manuel, K. (2008). *Practical research methods for librarians and information professionals*. New York: Neal-Schuman.

Cook, D. & Farmer, L. (Eds.), (2011). *Using qualitative methods in action research: How librarians can get to the why of data*. Chicago: Association of College and Research Libraries.

Powell, R. R., & Connaway, L. S. (2004). *Basic research methods for librarians* (4th ed.). Westport, CT: Libraries Unlimited, Greenwood.

Radford, M. (2011). Forward. In Douglas Cook & Lesley Farmer (Eds.), *Using qualitative methods in action research: How librarians can get to the why of data*. Chicago: Association of College and Research Libraries.

Sauermann, H., & Roach, M. (2013). Increasing Web survey response rates in innovation research: An experimental study of static and dynamic contact design features. *Research Policy, 42*, 273–286.

Shoaf, E. C. (2003). Using a professional moderator in library focus group research. *College and Research Libraries, 64*(2), 124–132.

Valentine, B. (1993). Undergraduate research behavior: Using focus groups to generate theory. *The Journal of Academic Librarianship, 19*(5), 300–304.

Zedeck, S. (Ed.), (2013). *APA dictionary of statistics and research methods*. Washington, DC: American Psychological Association.

Creating the marketing plan

4.1 Introduction

According to the Association of Research Libraries (ARL), marketing is the process of planning and executing such aspects of library services as the conception, pricing, and promotion of ideas, goods, and services to create interactions that will satisfy organizational objectives (Association of Research Libraries, 1999). To accomplish this goal, the first task is to understand and then to define the organization's objectives. The ARL says marketing collects and uses demographic, geographic, behavioral, and psychological information for this purpose. Marketing, they say, "inspires public awareness and educates" (Association of Research Libraries, 1999, p. 1).

But, why do it? According to Helinsky (2008), "if we, the representatives of libraries, do not act now to demonstrate how important we are, and how significant a resource we constitute for the whole of society, we will just not be noticed in the ongoing information flow" (p. 7). To remain "significant" and "noticed" is a continuous effort to encourage inspiration and develop life-long learning skills in the patrons. Library and librarian existence depends on creating and securing the loyalty of satisfied customers.

Libraries already often conduct market planning activities to secure organizational commitment for funding current library services and resources, to develop information projects, and to create marketing plans. Any organizational commitment is easier to obtain if the academic library market is educated. The constituencies responsible for funding our services and projects are our directors, vice presidents, deans, boards of directors, presidents, and any other administrative body that holds the library purse strings. They need to be cognizant of our current services, resources, and future plans, all of which are outlined in an effective marketing plan's executive summary. In many of these areas, keep in mind that librarians conduct market planning activities so that they can continue to secure funding and maintain budgetary stability in a *competitive* environment.

Marketing affects traditional perceptions and opinions of libraries and librarians. Libraries can benefit from following business models that provide or incorporate consulting services. Murphy (2011) states that librarians should learn from their examples. "Businesses recognize consultants' value because consultants consistently deliver results while communicating their value to the constituents they serve" (p. 3).

Librarians should consider the bigger picture. Marketing is not only promotions. "What is below the surface… includes important strategic components such as evaluating the needs of the customer; planning the various elements of the mix in order to answer those needs; and periodically evaluating the results" (Gupta & Savard, 2010, p. 3553).

We face other marketing challenges as well. "Librarians often mistake marketing as advertising and publicity, which are just two of the many tools or tactics in the marketing arsenal" (Murphy, 2011, p. 39). Many librarians have not had any formal training or education in marketing and lack experience with marketing principles and implementation in academic libraries. In libraries, it is difficult to use the traditional business marketing models, based on the four P's of marketing: product, price, promotion, and place. For example, if libraries are not profit driven, and we follow a profit-driven model, how do we measure success? Marketing is also a complicated problem for libraries because of our wide range of products and services, and the measure of success might be the statistics used to document usage and attendance. For example, we measure the number of books circulated, interlibrary loan activity, and reference desk transactions.

Dealing with a variety of constituents is another challenge when market planning in a library. Academic constituents range from students to faculty and administrators to board members. We also need to consider a sometimes overlooked group: the library staff user. Mix in the special interest groups and the general public, and the gamut of inclusion increases. We need to reach all of these special groups, enticing them to use the products or services that best suit their needs.

The need to market plan is twofold: we need to increase awareness of services and resources, and we also need to better understand user needs and expectations. As mentioned, each group has their own set of unique needs and preferences. We want to and need to retain current patrons, while attracting future patrons. Academic library patrons are no longer our captive audiences, because they can access information via the often faster, easier, and more convenient Internet. Users might not realize it's inaccurate or outdated, or they might not care. If librarians can help the patrons understand how to limit their searches and evaluate the resources, then we are growing our patron base. Librarians have to market plan so that the general constituency better understands what the library offers, and thus develop a growing appreciation for the value of librarians.

The key elements of market planning most relevant to the academic library are:

Assessment tools—a method by which an instrument is used to gather data. Examples of marketing assessment tools include statistics, surveys, and focus groups. These tools should be used to collect data from all key constituencies. The data collected is used to understand the past, present, and future status of the organization.

Constituents: the people the academic library serves, who interact with our products and services. Academic library constituents might include students, faculty, campus staff, library staff, administrators, executives, community and area residents, visitors, alumni, and special interest groups, among others.

Facilitator—a person who leads a focus group to gather data from participants for the purpose of understanding user needs and expectations.

Focus group—group discussions held in a small, specially selected group, often to identify organizational problems or for market research purposes. The group usually comprises fewer than 15 participants and its members are selected for their relevance to the discussion topic. Discussions focus on a limited subject area and are guided by a moderator or facilitator. The discussions may be recorded via video or audio and may take place over a period of several months. Focus groups have become increasingly popular in politics for gaging public opinion (Focus Group, 2010).

Implementation schedule—sets timelines and due dates; analyzes work into project tasks; conducts research, including literature reviews, focus groups, and surveys.

Marketing: the process by which a library keeps abreast of constituent needs and desires, seeks to better understand user needs and desires, and incorporates products and services to meet those needs and desires.

Marketing plan: the systematic road map or plan of action that guides the marketing process.

Mission statement: a mission statement is written by an organization to define its objectives and aims. The mission statement communicates a company's intent to its stakeholders, including its customers, suppliers, and employees. For a company's employees, the mission statement provides daily guidance and provides a sense of comradery and common purpose.

Project charter—an outline of what the marketing team aims to complete. It will define the team charge and the task it is assigned.

Promotional tools: media and methods used to advertise and create interest in new library products and services. This includes educational materials and ongoing activities in advertising and public relations.

Sample promotional tools

Brochures
Whether it's a general library overview, or specific to ILL, Research Services, Bookmobiles, etc., have them professionally printed. Use a graphic artist who works on the library staff, or if not, one who works or studies on-campus. Interns are another great asset.

Publishing
Create a weekly or monthly newsletter, or add content to newsletters published by outside constituencies (student newspaper, community presses, campus publications, media press releases, bee newspapers).

Events
Guest speakers, resume writing, research training sessions...be creative, but serve patrons' needs and interests.

Outreach
Library instruction, computer training, guest lecturing/public speaking, and community meetings.

Strategic planning: "the continuous process of making present entrepreneurial (risk taking) decisions systematically and with the best possible knowledge of their futurity, organizing systematically the efforts needed to carry out these decisions, and measuring the results of these decisions against the expectations through organized, systematic feed-back" (Drucker, 1959).

SWOT analysis: breakdown of an organization into its strengths and weaknesses (the internal analysis), with an assessment of the opportunities open to it and the threats confronting it. Strengths and weaknesses are internal and affect the company in the present; opportunities and threats deal with external factors and the future. SWOT analysis is commonly used in marketing and strategic studies (SWOT analysis, 2014).

Vision statement: A statement giving a broad, aspirational image of the future an organization is aiming to achieve. Vision statements express corporate vision. They are related to mission statements (Vision Statement, 2009).

4.2 Components of a market plan for the academic library

According to Duke and Tucker (2007), a marketing plan is a living document that will "change and develop every year as an institution learns from past marketing activities, the needs and desires of users change, and services, programs and resources of the library evolve to meet those changing needs" (p. 54). Marketing plans vary in size and content, depending on the needs and preferences of the library preparing the plan. Each plan will, however, have several sections that provide a roadmap, from the beginning of the process, to the plans for continually assessing progress and subsequent results. An effective plan outlines each step, from where a library is to where it wants to be, with detailed directions provided along the way.

According to Summey (2004), a marketing plan "answers the following basic questions: Where is the organization at currently? Where does the organization want to ultimately go? And, how will the organization get there?" (p. 461). A marketing plan is more than just flyers, posters, Web site announcements, and bookmarks. Marketing is only a part of a strategic plan and it should incorporate the library mission and vision statements.

Marketing plans answer many questions, such as:

- Who are the constituents we need to reach?
- What do we do best, and what opportunities do we have to improve?
- What library staff will be responsible for creating and implementing the marketing plan?
- What resources and services will be created, deleted, or showcased?
- What are the standard promotional tools to be incorporated into the marketing plan?
- What assessment methods will be used and how often?

As each institution is unique, the documents created will vary, sometimes widely. However, most marketing plans will contain some or all of the following more detailed sections:

1. Table of contents
2. Executive summary
3. Introduction
4. Project charter statements
5. Marketing committee membership
6. Defined constituents
7. Mission and vision statements
8. SWOT analysis summary
9. Strategic plans—including immediate and long-range marketing opportunities and concerns

10. Implementation schedules
11. Assessment tools
12. Summaries
13. Appendices as needed

1. A table of contents will simply show the manner in which the work is organized. This is especially helpful for senior administrators who may need to quickly navigate through a library team's entire work, looking perhaps for only executive summary and implementation schedules. They can consult the table of contents and find the needed information and documentation within, quickly and easily.
2. Executive summaries are written with the senior administrators in mind. They provide a concise overview of the marketing project. The executive summary is often considered the most important section of a marketing plan because it will attract and entice administrators and will therefore strengthen their commitment and support for the library's projects.

    According to the SBA, in the business world, "this section briefly tells your reader where your company is, where you want to take it, and why your business idea will be successful. If you are seeking financing, the executive summary is also your first opportunity to grab a potential investor's interest. The executive summary should highlight the strengths of your overall plan and therefore be the last section you write. However, it usually appears first in your business plan document" (Executive Summary).
3. The introduction will include a list of the market planning committee membership. It will introduce them and provide their job titles and any biographical data that the library marketing team deems relevant. Also introduce constituency lists, including library staff members, and include the demographics that readers should know. For example, list the number of enrolled graduate students versus enrolled undergraduate students, with the percentage each represents out of the total student population. Consider also creating charts that break out numbers of students per course of study, with corresponding percentages of the entire student population. It might be also helpful for readers to see the similar statistics for other constituents, such as campus employees or faculty.
4. Mission and vision statements tell the readers where the organization is and where it plans to go: the present versus the future. Mission and vision are our guiding principles. A mission statement performs a general public relations function. It states the reason the library exists, and details its key activities and functions. It educates patrons on library resources, services, and overall value to the community. Most importantly, mission statements create support from our audience of patrons, staff, volunteers, donors, trustees, and administrative personnel. A mission statement can set the organizational tone for library staff as well. The library staff are, after all, customers of one another. The mission will enable the staff to focus on the reason they are there.

Although writing a mission statement can be demanding and complex, employing the following can be helpful:

- Use clear and narrow terms to concisely state the library purpose.
- List some of the library's most *significant* services and resources.
- Circulate the mission statement to all library staff. Also invite input. Host a staff or constituent meeting to engage participation and ideas.
- Be creative! Brainstorm!

- Get final approval from senior administrators.
- Circulate the final mission statement to all staff in the library and/or its system libraries.

Although writing a mission statement can be demanding and complex, using clear and specific terms to concisely state the libraries purpose can be helpful. Invite input. The more people given the chance to review the drafts, the better the result. Not only does this create buy in, but it also enhances the overall statement. So host a staff or constituent meeting to engage participation and ideas. Circulate the draft mission statement to all staff in the library(ies). Be creative and use constructive brainstorming activities. Staff comments can feed off other comments and lead to outstanding results. It is important to get a final seal of approval from the institution's administrators. The administration can accelerate approval of the statement so that the institution's presidential council can review it also. After the final mission statement has been approved, proudly post it to the library Web site.

A vision statement clearly outlines where the library strives to be. It is in many aspects a glimpse into the future. Rutgers University Libraries have an insightful mission and vision statement available at: http://www.libraries.rutgers.edu/mission.

5. SW OT analysis and summary: Each marketing plan begins with a through in-house SWOT analysis. A SWOT analysis is generated after an organization conducts both a self-assessment and a user-assessment. It is the process of uncovering underlying strengths (S), weaknesses (W), opportunities (O), and threats (T). This involves an analysis of the library's internal operations and its external forces. When writing a SWOT consider the following questions:

    Strengths (internal forces)
    What are the advantages the library brings to the academic community?
    What does the academic community think are the library's strengths? Use focus group data to guide and confirm this analysis.
    Has the library been complimented or received any positive publicity regarding any aspect of the operations by the academic community?
    Weaknesses (internal forces)
    Has the library received negative feedback? Again, gather and use focus group data.
    What can be improved?
    Do the library staff experience roadblocks in work processes?
    What processes break down?
    Opportunities (external forces)
    What have the patrons been asking for?
    What new programs or services can the library create?
    Is the campus growing in such a way that presents opportunities?
    What new products are library vendors creating?
    What new industry standards or mandates are emerging?
    Threats (external forces)
    What new industry standards or mandates are emerging?
    Who are the competitors?
    What are competitors doing better than the library?
    What are competitors offering?
    What new products are being created by library vendors? (Note that these can be an opportunity or a threat).

Creating the marketing plan

The following chart outlines some sample ideas to incorporate into a SWOT analysis.

Strengths: What does the library do well? • Popular library instruction program. • Administrative support.	Opportunities: What library resources and services can be improved? What new services and resources can be offered? • Interlibrary loan can be streamlined and turn-around time can be improved.
Weaknesses: What areas or services put us at risk or make us vulnerable? • Increased use of Google Scholar, which is perceived to be superior to subscription-based library databases.	Threats: Who are the library's key competitors, and what lies on the horizon in the twenty-first century? • Google-based search engines. • Patron driven acquisitions versus skilled librarian collection development.

6. Goals and objectives can include both immediate and long-term goals. Some organizations choose to create 5-year strategic plans, and most of that data can be encapsulated into this section. As part of this section, include a promotional plan of action. This will guide the library team to successfully outline what to promote—for example, a new dormitory-reference desk. It will provide a corresponding implementation schedule (see next point). Effectively, say what to promote and when to promote it. The goals and objectives will also help create implementation schedules.
7. Implementation schedules have various components, including, but not limited to, action, goal, date to begin, date to end, responsible staff member(s), and cost. A schedule can be created as a Gantt chart, using project management software like MS Project, or simply within an Excel spreadsheet or Word Chart. A quick Google search on "Gantt Chart" will provide several examples of such.
8. Assessment tools: How did the team gather data and how and when do they plan to reassess the progress they have made through their market planning and promotional efforts? In "Using data to engage, motivate and affect change" (2005), Denise Troll Covey says that, "presumably, a culture of assessment is a set of beliefs, behaviors, and assumptions that drive an ongoing cycle of data gathering, analysis, interpretation, organization, presentation, and use to achieve planned objectives." She continues to say, "Libraries aim to use data to demonstrate their contribution and accountability, to identify problems or potential solutions, to monitor or facilitate improvement, and to provide evidence of need" (p. 83). Documenting this effectively will help reduce the rate of collecting what Covey calls "orphaned data." "Orphaned data and knowledge waste resources, reduce the benefits of the effort invested to acquire them, raise costs, veil challenges, obstruct opportunities, and hurt morale" (p. 83). It is also important to clearly state what issues need to be addressed in order to design questions that will generate the best data possible. The best data is that which illustrates the library's case and generates financial and procedural support from senior administrators.
9. The summary will conclude the work, adding any special notes and describing data yet to be documented. It can be a simple bulleted list, a few paragraphs of essay-based text, or a diagram. The best summary will reflect the skills and talents of the team. Librarians must put their best foot forward here, as many busy senior administrators will only glace the market plan, but will focus on this summary, in addition to the executive summary that appears at the beginning of the marketing plan.

10. Appendices can include survey results and focus group themes and comments. Comments and themes are valuable qualitative data and information that can be used to assess and explore constituent concerns verbatim, and as spoken by the patron.

4.3 Conclusion

According to Duke and Tucker (2007), a marketing plan is a living document that will "change and develop every year as an institution learns from past marketing activities, the needs and desires of users change, and services, programs and resources of the library evolve to meet those changing needs" (p. 54).

Through this valuable process, the library gains an opportunity to in fact harness twenty-first century concerns to further its mission, rather than reacting in an unplanned way to the threats these technological and modern day changes seem to present. The effective market plan allows the library to thoughtfully evolve as a relevant player in the digital information age.

4.4 Exercises

1. Please review the following academic library mission statement and discuss how it meets the general criteria for mission statements. Revise, making improvement suggestions.
   - "Our Library" actively participates in the education of students, and supports the research and curricular needs of the entire college community. "Our Library" fosters academic excellence and academic freedom by providing access to a broad spectrum of information in the curriculum supported by the College's overriding mission and vision for the future.
2. Create a vision statement for the library where you work or study.
3. Who would you include on a team to create the mission and vision statements, and create the SWOT analysis? Why?

References

Association of Research Libraries. (1999). SPEC Flyer 240.
Covey, D. T. (2005). Using data to persuade: State your case and prove it. *Library Leadership and Management, 19*(2), 82–89.
Drucker, P. F. (1959). Long-range planning-challenge to management science. *Management Science, 5*(3), 238–249.
Duke, L. M., & Tucker, T. (2007). How to develop a marketing plan for an academic library. *Technical Services Quarterly, 25*(1), 51–68.
Executive Summary. http://www.sba.gov/content/business-plan-executive-summary Retrieved 29.10.14.
Focus Group. (2010). The Hutchinson unabridged encyclopedia with atlas and weather guide. Retrieved from http://www.credoreference.com/entry/heliconhe/focus_group.

Gupta, D., & Savard, R. (2010). Marketing library and information services. In M. Bates & M. Maack (Eds.), *Encyclopedia of library and information services* (pp. 3553–3560). Boca Raton: CRC Press.

Helinsky, Z. (2008). *A short-cut to marketing the library*. Oxford: Chandos Publishing Limited.

Murphy, S. A. (2011). *The library as information consultant: Transforming reference for the information age*. Chicago: American Library Association.

Summey, T. (2004). If you build it will they come? Creating a marketing plan for distance learning library services. *Journal of Library Administration, 41*(3/4), 459–470.

SWOT Analysis. (2014). The Hutchinson unabridged encyclopedia with atlas and weather guide. Retrieved from http://www.credoreference.com/entry/heliconhe/swot_analysis.

Vision Statement. (2009). Business: The ultimate resource. Retrieved from http://www.credoreference.com/entry/ultimatebusiness/vision_statement.

Project control—Managing marketing initiatives

5

5.1 Introduction

Even the most carefully and thoughtfully created marketing plan cannot implement itself. That would be quite the magical feat! Understanding aspects of project control will first take the mystery out of creating a marketing plan. It will also help the twenty-first century librarian use the data gathered, the ideas generated, and the decisions made in developing a library marketing plan, taking it from the research and planning stage, to the implementation stage. Project management and control are keys to creating, organizing, and implementing a marketing plan. Effective management also then provides a structure for successfully selecting initiatives, organizing events and activities, and identifying responsibilities.

For example, in organizing the overall marketing plan, librarians and marketing team members may define key initiatives, and create a schedule by which they will be prioritized. Then the team can outline key tasks to be completed: the macroplanning stage. When these initiatives are identified, for example creating a faculty in-servicing program, the project management principles can again help the team organize and delegate tasks for implementation, while setting deadline dates and tracking potential expenses.

In my book chapter, *Project management in libraries: An overview for middle managers*, I wrote, "A *project* is any event that is planned and managed. Projects sometimes affect only one department for which the project manager is responsible. Other times, the project affects more than one department or even many departments within a library" (2011, p. 211). The success of the project depends on the process of formally managing it from inception to completion, whether it is the overall marketing plan, or the individual initiatives or promotional efforts. Each project should be systematically controlled throughout its duration. Again, the library team must manage the marketing plan as a project as much as the individual data-driven initiatives selected.

How do we do this given the basic fact that librarians with college degrees in the humanities or social sciences, or those who have never worked outside the librarian's profession, are often unfamiliar with project control principles and techniques? These principles are often not covered in library science programs, certainly not in the detail needed once active in the profession. This expertise may also be an organization-specific; some library or college leadership entities are in tune with project control practices, they may provide guidance in this area. Librarians who do not find this support might shy away from practicing project control. However, once librarians learn key project management principles, they can share their knowledge and expertise with their colleagues. I've previously written, "the first project run using project management techniques can serve as a modeling tool for all future project plans" (Lucas, 2011, p. 212).

Project control is the process by which a marketing plan is managed and implemented. Specifically, this applies to the individual promotional events, or initiatives, where key services and resources are added, enhanced and/or improved, according to both the mission and the marketing plan. As such, project control is an effective method for managing, planning, and implementing. Oftentimes, when a project is controlled, a selected team of librarians and/or staff will systematically and strategically plan for the actions needed for each segment of the marketing plan to be successfully implemented.

Leaders who create market plans may also serve as *project managers*. As such, they are responsible for managing the overall marketing plan as well as some of the individual initiatives or miniprojects that comprise the *marketing portfolio*. In the marketing plan, they will have to plan and manage the overall endeavor and assist others who are given the responsibility of managing their own implementation.

A project portfolio is one tool that a project manager can incorporate in a strategic implementation plan. According to Jennifer Vinopal (2012), a *project portfolio* will outline in registry format all of the projects to be implemented as part of an overall plan (p. 380). Project portfolio management (PPM), she says, "is a continual or iterative process that allows organizations to observe what is happening in the present and to analyze and learn from the past to better plan for the future. Rather than thinking about projects as works silos, when we review the project inventory we look holistically at the portfolio and are very attentive to relationships and interdependencies among initiatives (such as common resources, deliverable, or workflows)" (p. 382). Vinopal also provides examples: in the portfolio, she says, "It's easy to find answers to questions like:...'At what point over the coming year will our workload lighten enough for us to take on new projects?'" (p. 382). PPM is also good for understanding whether projects are finishing late, or whether staff are overcommitted.

The project initiatives will reflect the overall strategic goals in what we can call an "umbrella marketing plan." Start project management at the beginning, using the following simplified events:

1. Create the mission, then the vision statements.
2. Conduct SWOT analysis.
3. Conduct assessments, conduct literature reviews, and then analyze the data.
4. Decide on the library's most important goals and prioritize actions using the project management principles.
5. Be open and flexible. If needed, change the plan or the direction as the process progresses.

As discussed in previous chapters, an umbrella marketing plan begins by examining, and if necessary rewriting, the library mission and vision statement. These statements must also directly relate to the institutional mission and vision. For example, if the institution is developing a series of online programs, the library mission is to equally and effectively serve the needs of all patrons, remote or on campus. If marketing assessments and research show that the library's patrons (and administrators) want a document delivery or virtual reference service, then librarians may develop a plan that will meet the expectations of these marketing project goals.

Authors Zhang and Bishop (2005) say that "the objectives that typify the key function for project management...include the ability to assess the overall requirements for the project, track tasks, allocate resources, and share information" with shareholders (p. 148). They also say that in their experience in implementing virtual reference, the project plan they created enabled them to "assemble all of the task information in a core file with estimated completion dates and additional task-related information" (p. 148). This helps team members "manage tasks, track deadlines, schedule staff, and share up-to-date information with stakeholders" (p. 148). Tasks that have to be completed in a successive order are called "dependency relationships" (p. 148).

As such, the tasks need to be completed in succession for proper implementation of your project. Project control ensures that everyone stays informed, organized, and focused. Project control also enables managers and team members to effectively and efficiently meet their goals.

In a separate and specific promotional section of the marketing plan, several initiatives will likely be outlined to support the mission and vision of the organization and library, and in response to assessments (that is, survey and focus group data). Each individual initiative is itself a project that should be managed in a systematically controlled manner. This ensures several positive results: it coordinates staff and librarian efforts, decreases chance of overlap and rework, and keeps the team on track. It also allows the staff and librarians who are not on the marketing team to see and understand what is happening, why, by whom, and when. Providing this planned communication with nonteam members will increase the chance that they will buy into the new services or resources. In other words, they will support and invest in the outcomes. They will also be more supportive and participatory when it's time to implement the project if they understand what will happen, why and how.

The purposes and benefits of project control techniques are straightforward. Librarians should use these techniques because they help organize goals as well as the necessary tasks to achieve them; additionally they will ensure that managers and upper administrative leaders understand and share these common goals. Projects are successfully implemented when the plans, objectives, and outcomes are agreed upon. Additionally, project control guides the process of inception, implementation, and completion in an efficient, expert, and cost effective manner.

5.2 Taming a potential beast

In project control, there needs to be a *project charter*. As defined in Chapter 4, a marketing plan project charter is "an outline of what the marketing team will complete. It will define your team charge and the tasks you are assigned. Project charters set the tone and sometimes the pace that is needed to complete its charge."

According to Webb (2001), a charter outlines a project manager's responsibilities, and the individual role in the project manager plays in the day-to-day implementation of the plan. To ensure that each task is completed in the proper order, and that all staff are responsible for completing their assigned tasks, the project plan will also include a list of the necessary resources for each task or task group. For example, if a team wants to implement document delivery, first they need to assess the need for such, and analyze the results. It is not enough for a librarian or a staff member to say students want this without actually knowing for sure, using student-generated data. And before the library can begin making photocopies and delivering them to the students, the team needs to be sure that sufficient equipment and staff are available to complete the work on a daily basis. Therefore, researching and pricing equipment needs is a line item in an effective project control plan.

Having these mechanisms in place will help prevent the chances of necessary activities falling through the cracks, while also ensuring that tasks are being completed. The activities necessary for success might include obtaining materials, directing staff, conducting training, and purchasing needed equipment. Even if the manager is not taking part in the day-to-day activities and tasks, Webb (2001) continues to say, he or she will have daily involvement in ensuring that the project goes forward smoothly. Each project can be a component of the plan, not identical to the plan itself. In other words, project control will help in implementing service/resource improvement plans and the corresponding promotional activities.

Keller (2001) says project management, or design, as he calls it, shares several common elements (p. 10). He also says that there is a "clear goal, an outline of how to achieve the goal." There needs to also be a mission, level of energy and discipline to complete the project, he said. Accordingly, I agreed, "the mission statement includes goals and objectives, deliverables, costs, and any other information needed to define the team's charge and goal. These parameters include timeliness, cost effectiveness, and quality. A team must meet their expectations on time and under a defined budget" (Lucas, 2010, p. 212).

As I have previously published, in a book chapter on project management for middle managers (2011), the following outline can guide anyone through a project control, specifically in regards to managing both the marketing plan and its individual initiatives. These should be formally managed to solicit participation and support from staff members, both within and outside of the immediate marketing team.

1. Define the project (marketing vs. an initiative, such as launching virtual reference services)
    a. Project charter—or goal summary statement
    b. Timeline (which may be ongoing so be clear about the deadlines)
    c. Benefits/challenges
    d. Overall materials budget
    e. Suggested team members
2. Seek out a *Project Champion or Project Sponsor*—a senior member of the library staff or administration (director or CIO if needed) to become the team's cheerleader and continually support the process
3. Propose a project charter or summary to senior management
4. After project approval, finalize and invite team members selected for implementation
5. Analyze work into tasks
    a. Create task lists using project management software (Figures 5.1 Gantt Chart and 5.2 MS Project)

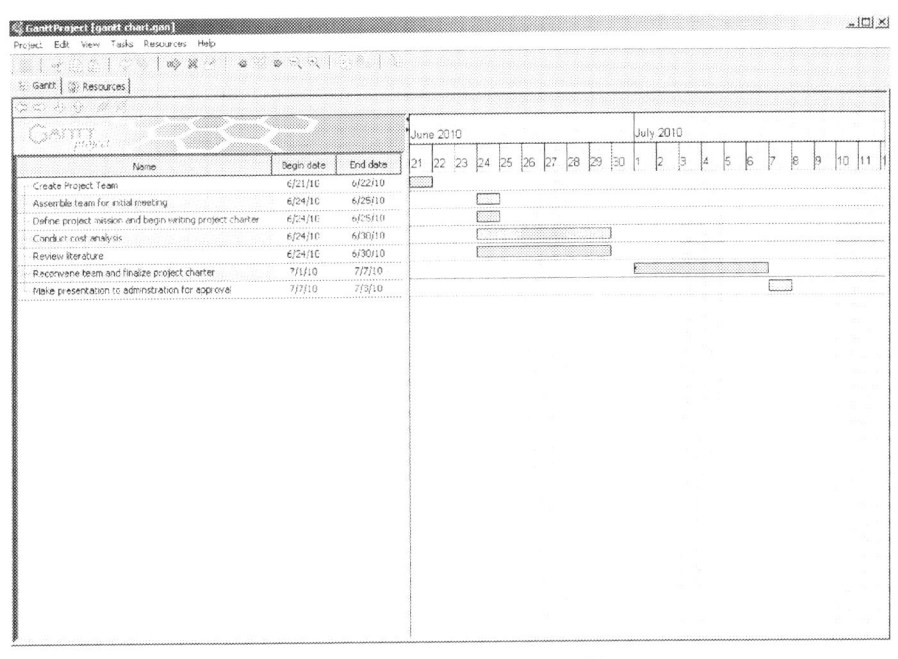

Project control—Managing marketing initiatives 45

Figure 5.1 Lucas project management for middle managers (2011).

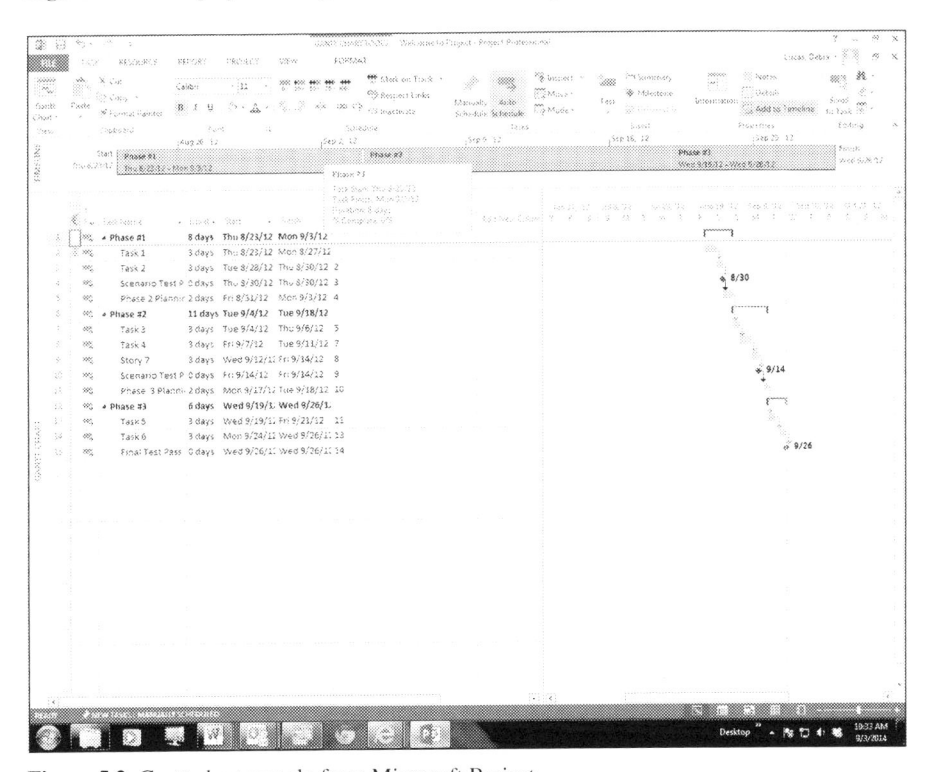

Figure 5.2 Gantt chart sample from Microsoft Project.

b. Organize tasks into sequential order
   c. Discuss technical issues and training issues
   d. List materials needed and create a review budget
   e. Plan for project pilot program
   f. Initiate pilot program
   g. Reassess progress, outstanding strengths, opportunities for improvement, comments, and themes
   h. Create policy and procedure documentation
   i. Obtain permission to launch
   j. Launch project
   k. Reassess
   l. Revise project charter as needed
   m. Provide status updates to senior management as needed
   n. Define timeframe for future project tasks as needed.

Effective project design and control includes a written project summary, including some or all of the following components:

- an introduction
- an official team charge
- project parameters
- a list of team member tasks with deadline dates
- a budget or cost analysis
- a list of the staff required to implement or launch the project, including those not on the project team
- a training plan
- a timelines
- a summary and assessment method.

5.3 The unexpected turns: Change management

Different teams would naturally run the same project differently. For a project to be successful, the team needs to understand that if necessary, plans can change mid-implementation. Wong (2007) writes: "All team members want the same thing (to achieve the project goals), but each goes after it differently due to their diversity" (p. 17). Wong also says that "team behaviors are the collective behaviors of individual team members. Individual behaviors are formed by internal factors—the human factors that make us unique: our genetics, values, personalities, experience, culture, and beliefs" (p. 19).

Ideally, as the marketing team is assembled and as work progresses, people are cooperating, generating creative ideas, and implementing change according to schedule. However, as Tricia Kelly (2010) points out, "some library and information management (LIM) professionals see change as stressful and as anything but a positive adventure" (p. 163). She says that "change is a constant for LIM professionals whether it is to do with the technology we use, the technology we assist our clients to use, with aspects of the physical library, or with the evolving nature of the professional role itself" (p. 163).

The challenge in project control is to inspire and excite the staff, not alienate them due to the stress associated with change. *Appreciative inquiry* (AI), as described by Kelly (2010), is a technique by which change management is based on highlighting the best an organization is, instead of the best it can become, "building on those positive experiences" (p. 164). This form of positive change management looks for opportunities to grow and improve on what is good, instead of focusing on an organization's shortcomings.

When faced with change, employees might ask themselves what impact the change will have on their work life. According to Jennifer Bull (2002), it is challenging to turn the negative into a positive. We must recognize the challenges inherent in asking "How can I effectively change?" or "What changes can I make to produce effective results?" (p. 11). She observes, however, that these challenges can be turned into positive opportunities for growth. "While organizational change is usually initiated at administrative levels, it is important for staff at all levels to gain a sense of ownership in orchestrated changes" (p. 12). "A supervisor can do a lot to encourage positive attitudes in relation to change by building incentives, setting the pace, and teaching reluctant personnel how to speak out during brainstorming or planning session" (p. 12). "Constant growth brings constant change" (p. 12).

According to Lubans (2010), in *Leaving the Comfort Zone*, "An organization's well-being and growth develops in the learning zone—the organization stagnates in the comfort zone" (p. 154). He says there are risks of both success and of failure in the learning zone, but the risk is within our control—"we are almost always up to the challenge, and we have the ability to solve the problem provided that we care enough to make the extra effort" (p. 155).

In fact, change can produce unexpected outcomes. Often we forget that at the end of the project the implementation process itself is change. "Whether the expected outcomes were initially met with skepticism, excitement or even derision, those outcomes are about be realized" (Somani, 2014, p. 70). Dealing with change management is challenging. During implementation, even those once enthusiastic about the project might have a change of heart, especially if unanticipated problems emerge during implementation. According to Somani, this is a real shock to project managers. To prepare, she says, remind everyone why the project exists. She also recommends creating training and support guidelines and manuals to assist with the conversion of resources or services.

To assist those affected by change, the twenty-first century librarian must also lead by example. Positive changes breed positive changes. If feelings and concerns fester, negativity is the surest outcome. Negative feelings, once developed, will then become a barrier to implementing changes. The academic library is traditionally a top-down culture, so if project managers or project sponsors demonstrate stress or negativity, it will trickle down. Try to keep all managers and staff on board to avoid a toxic change environment. According to Cooperrider (1997), "Organizations are centers of human readiness…and relationships thrive where there is an appreciative eye—when people see the best in one another, when they can share their dreams and ultimately concerns in affirming ways, and when they are connected in full voice to create not just new worlds but better worlds" (p. 1). Forming partnerships, as discussed in Chapter 6, is imperative to change management. Library staff members are customers of one another, and should therefore exist and produce as partners with a common goal.

Remember, project sponsors are also cheerleaders, so look to them to rally the troops as needed. The library's key constituents in the change management process are its internal customers, after all. They need to become cheerleaders and ambassadors when the new program or service is rolled out so that they can diffuse any conflict with the rest of our constituents. They need to be not only supportive of the change; they need to be supported *throughout* the change as well. Attitudinal shifts that occur during the change process must be acknowledged.

5.4 Discussion questions

1. List five potential stakeholders in project management. Who might serve on a project management team? List job titles or departments.
2. What elements might comprise your project summary (that which is delivered to senior management and administrators)?
3. What data does a project charter contain?

5.5 A library's tale—Case study

A student expresses concerns with the current Interlibrary Loan program. "What? I waited a week for my articles, just like you said. I'm here to pick them up and now you say I have overdue fines so you didn't process my requests at all. Now I have to wait even longer? Why didn't someone tell me sooner?"

Another student sends in a request for a journal article the library owns. An e-mail is generated that gives the student instructions for obtaining the article from the print collection. First, the instructions overwhelm the patron, who is told to purchase a photocopy card, then find the journal, and then photocopy the article. To further complicate matters, the patron is a distance education student who never goes to the campus for class and lives 30 miles away. What next?

These real-life scenarios occurred in real time at a small private library in Buffalo, NY, in the year 2006. It was a time before the Montante Family Library at D'Youville College (enrollment 2600 students) created a home-grown online request process to ease student dissatisfaction (prior to implementing ILLiad). It was a time of tension between librarians and disgruntled students. In that tumultuous time in ILL history, all students would have to enter the library, write bibliographic information on a paper form, and then come back in approximately a week to see if their articles had arrived.

In addition to comments made to librarians at the library research and interlibrary loan desks, a marketing team conducted an electronic survey that found students were not entirely happy with the program. The survey results suggest that they would prefer better, faster, and more convenient services, such as document delivery and e-mail or tracking notifications.

The marketing team then solicited input from librarians, staff, and the library director. These findings indicated the stakeholders were enthusiastic to explore their options in creating a better ILL service. Using the library mission and vision statements as a guiding force, the marketing team then agreed to work on this initiative as a separate and unique project.

The librarians found a project sponsor to grant them the permission needed to create a work team to address the problems faced by students and librarians in the ILL department. The head of interlibrary loan served as the project control manager, selecting two of the four part-time interlibrary loan librarians to become team members; the library director served as the project sponsor.

Their first step was to review the mission statements of the interlibrary loan department, the library and the college. The team then defined the mission of this project using a project charter. With this accomplished, some project team members conducted a literature review while others embarked on a fact-finding mission. For example, they conducted informal telephone surveys to determine how other, similar college libraries were handling these kinds of situations. They created an online survey for ILL users, and also conducted interviews with key stakeholders, such as front-line public service staff. Finally, after much debate and hours analyzing the data they generated, they created a service improvement plan to be submitted to the sponsor and senior administration.

As a result of the literature review, team planning, and administrative approval, the librarians implemented the use of electronic submissions forms generated by e-mail exchanges. After they implemented these improvements, students became able to place e-mail requests from any Internet-connected computer. The team also incorporated a system using e-mail notifications to inform students whether a request has technical issues or could not be filled for procedural reasons. For example, if a student has fines, overdue books, or requests an item that the library owns, the librarians notify them immediately by e-mail. The librarians also created a process to notify students via e-mail alerts when their items arrive.

Over the course of the next year or so, the librarians studied their results. Their reassessment consisted of conducting more user satisfaction surveys and performing an analysis of department statistics. Their findings: students are increasingly more satisfied with the service and they use it more often. Good word is spreading and administration is pleased with the rave reviews.

5.6 Practice case study questions

1. What service issues did the librarians and the patrons experience?
2. What charge can be issued to the team?
3. What project control steps can this library take in preparing for change?
4. From the above passage, write a project charter. Who might become a project sponsor? What data is used to assess the success of their project control?

References

Bull, J. (2002). Managing the emotional side of change. *Library Mosaics*, *13*, 11–12.
Cooperrider, D. L. (1997). Resources for getting appreciative inquiry started: An example of OD proposal. *OD Practitioner*, *28*(1), 1–7.

Keller, J. R. (2001). Design, mission and inspiration. *Joys, Winter*, 10–12.
Kelly, T. (2010). A positive approach to change: The role of appreciative inquiry in library and information organizations. *Australian Academic and Research Libraries, 41*(3), 163–177.
Lubans, J. (2010). *Leading from the middle and other contrarian essays on library leadership.* Santa Barbara, CA: Libraries Unlimited/ABC-CLIO.
Lucas, D. (2010). Project management in libraries: An overview for middle managers. In T. Diamond (Ed.), *Middle management in academic and public libraries.* Santa Barbara, CA: Libraries Unlimited.
Somani, S. (2014). Cheerleading change. *PM Network, 5*, 70.
Vinopal, J. (2012). Project portfolio management for academic libraries: A gentle introduction. *College and Research Libraries, 7*, 379–389.
Webb, S. (2001). Project management in library and information services. *Information Management Report, 11*, 16–19.
Wong, Z. (2007). *Human factors in project management: Concepts, tools, and techniques for inspiring teamwork and motivation.* San Francisco: Jossey-Bass.
Zhang, Y., & Bishop, C. (2005). Project management tools for libraries: A planning and implementation model using Microsoft project. *Information Technology and Libraries, 11*, 147–152.

Partnerships

6.1 Partnership opportunities and constituencies (POC—Pronounced "poke")

A partnership represents the union between like-minded people, groups, or organizations who wish to reach a common goal or objectives. Often times, partners agree on a method to compensate one another, be it in perks, services, or wages. This chapter will introduce the basic premises of POC, with emphasis on the key constituent with whom a library can coordinate partnering efforts.

A *constituent* is a group of persons involved with, participating with, or being served by an organization. In an academic institution, constituents range from students, faculty, and staff, to campus administrators, the general public and local businesses. Libraries also serve such groups as their alumnus and donors.

Libraries who want to partner with other campus organizations can create advocates and library supporters, and ultimately improve the image of libraries, reinforce their importance to a college campus, and create a more positive impression of the librarians who manage the building, its resources and services. In fact, as the image of the library improves, and statistics for the use of library services and resources rise, then the financial and "emotional" support for the libraries increases. For example, regarding the research services department, Cassell and Hiremath (2013, p. 374) say that "collaborating with colleagues, users and individuals and entities outside the library is a good way for reference librarians to optimize their effectiveness." Additionally, they say:

> RUSA's competency guideline states that in the reference interview, users should be treated as partners or collaborators. Working effectively with colleagues within the institution as part of a team is another element of collaboration. Forming relationships with colleagues both inside and outside the profession can lead to mutually beneficial improvement in service and access (p. 374).

According to Bell (2009), organizational success is increasingly dependent on effective internal partnerships as organizations become more complex and as customer demands for improved service make excellence in communication and coordination a necessity. Cassell and Hiremath also say that relationship marketing goes beyond the traditional marketing methods, to "developing interactive programs that highlight individual staff expertise to cater to specific user needs." This technique is excellent for reference librarians because it allows long-term partnerships based on listening closely to our users (p. 397).

6.2 From constituents to partners—Forging the way

There are many methods for inviting constituents to become library partners. The following section discusses constituent groups and some means by which we can forge partnership relations. Groups inclusive for partnering will include students, faculty, staff, and administration. However, the academic library may also include outside communications staff, service offices, locational groups, community organizations, alumni, and donors in its arsenal of partnerships. Each group will be in the discussed in the following sections.

6.2.1 Partnering with students

Student partnerships are valuable because such a relationship exposes the library to students on a peer to peer level. Initiatives such as recruiting student ambassadors, and enlisting media studies students and university newspaper writers or radio broadcasters as library partners, will enable us to form lasting relationships with the student bodies. To do so, we need a complete marketing plan, full of the details, ideas, and timelines required to make the transition to a twenty-first century library. Ours must be a proactive profession.

When we partner with students, student groups become better aware of what we offer and why we offer it. Their support is as valuable as the support we receive from other constituents, such as the faculty. The partnership opportunities and constituencies (POC) create an atmosphere where students teach other students. Our partnerships opens doors to educating in innovative ways, by means we might not have considered in the past.

Student opinions are expressed most commonly by word of mouth, which is a very powerful promotional method. Satisfied students will sing praises to other students and faculty in conversation. However, students also complete exit interviews and surveys where administration collect satisfaction data, so if students are pleased or not, administration will know.

Case study: Drexel University's personal librarian program

Drexel University in Philadelphia, Pennsylvania, is a comprehensive global research university with 25,500 total students. Drexel is a ranked among the top 100 universities in the nation, and it is one of America's 15 largest private universities. Drexel has committed to being the nation's most civically engaged university, with community partnerships integrated into every aspect of service and academics. For more information, see http://www.drexel.edu/about/glance/.

Its downtown campus is the home to the Hagerty Library; the university also has a law and a health sciences library. Notably, Drexel also offers a "bookless" Library Learning Terrace, a 3000-square-foot library structure that opened on June 3, 2011. This location partners with other organization offices, such as the Learning Center. Bookless, says Danuto Nitecki, PhD. Dean of Libraries, is not the best term to use. She refers to it as "book-full" because they have both print and electronic books to share, according to her report in *Library Connect* (2012), available at http://libraryconnect.elsevier.com/articles/best-practices/2012-07/drexel-s-learning-terrace-enables-collaborative-learning-experience.

Nancy Bellafante is the coordinator of the personal librarian program at Hagerty. The focus of the program is on acclimating first-year students to academic libraries. At Drexel, the librarians inform first year students what they offer at the library and that creates a more positive impression and therefore a better experience with library. The librarians understand that first impressions are important (personal interview with Nancy Bellafante). This program was created to address three specific problems: students don't know librarians can help them, students prefer to ask friends instead, and students suffer from library anxiety. Currently, the school enjoys the presence of 14,202 traditional undergraduate students and many of those who started in Personal Librarian program have remained involved as they continue their studies. All incoming undergraduate students are now enrolled in the program.

In 2011, Kilzer wrote about the program, saying it was "meant to meet two objectives. First, by contacting new students from the beginning of their academic careers, the Libraries are better poised to be a proactive and reputable partner in a student's education and scholarship. Second, having received person-to-person correspondence from the library, a student may be more likely to think of the library as a place that has both useful resources and friendly, helpful people who can provide assistance with projects as needed" (Kilzer, 2011, p. 295). She continues to explain that at the inception of this program, 26 librarians and paraprofessional staff contacted approximately 2800 incoming freshman at Drexel. The Personal Librarian program, spearheaded by Beth Ten Have, piloted the service by mailing letters introducing each student to his or her Personal Librarian. In this partnership, a month before students started school in Fall 2010 quarter they received a letter at home describing the role librarians can play in a student's academic experience. Additional letters and e-mails were sent out each quarter with reminders and other pertinent information. More information about this program can be found on the Drexel University Library Web site at http://www.library.drexel.edu/about/programs.

MY PERSONAL LIBRARIAN
Engaging incoming Drexel students with library services through personal connections with staff.

Drexel University Libraries

6.2.2 Student faculty relations—Library advocates

Sometimes, we need to recruit students to get our message across. They can become our advocates, even champions. For example, in our attempt to enlighten faculty to the benefit of using traditional library services, such as a research desk or an instruction session, it may be more beneficial to use creative student generated methods. Mathews (2009) recommends creating a video and passing that onto one student, who can in turn forward it to other students. With student validity, it holds more merit. If one student found it helpful, so will others.

Just as the students forwarded it to one another, they will also share the video, and the experience, with their professors. Any business model holds that good service breeds good recommendations and positive reviews, and also generates repeat customers. This will increase the chances that students or faculty members will tell other students or faculty members to utilize the library's resources. Conversely, if there is a negative experience, that word will spread as well. "Relationships are the key to successful communication programs. This sentiment is echoed throughout the marketing literature, where it is often stated that the emotional connection that a person feels toward products, places, or services is what truly distinguishes these items" (Mathews, 2009, p. 73).

6.2.3 Ambassadors

We can use student ambassadors to help us uncover what is cool and trendy on campus, for example, if the student body is looking at our library Facebook and Twitter feeds. Also, they can help us outline upcoming trends that we can embrace, in the name of providing the best resources and services possible.

Mathews also defines ways to further help us understand the best ways to recruit these students:

- Identifying student leaders
- Advertising such positions in campus newspaper articles
- Posting information on academic Web sites
- Establishing a presence on the social Web
- Distributing feedback forms
- Creating assessment projects
- Obtaining their permission to promote their service recommendations

Other methods by which we can enlist students include reaching out to those students who have contacted us via research desk and interlibrary loan (ILL) e-mail queues. We know who they are and what the transaction was like. If the interaction was positive, capitalize on that. Reach out to those we do serve and involve them in ways that enable them to cheer on the library resources and services.

Other ideas include posting contact cards at key service desks and gaining exposure at open house events. We can try recruiting student government leaders, teaching assistants, and resident hall assistance to serve as library ambassadors. Welcome them into the library fold and train them so they understand the positive words to spread. Finally, librarians can enlist media students and specialists, such as campus student newspaper reporters, newsletter writers, and radio broadcasters.

Case study: University of Texas at San Antonio's Blue Crew

The libraries at the University of Texas at San Antonio (UTSA) are on the move. UTSA has three libraries: a main library, a downtown library, and a bookless library. Collectively, they house 1,224,000 books and 345 databases. The library has achieved great success in recent years, for example, in 2014, they were awarded the John Cotton Dana Library Public Relations Award (http://librarygrapevine.wordpress.com/may-2014/utsa-libraries-receives-john-cotton-dana-award/), one of the most prestigious awards granted by the American Library Association. This success comes just a few years after Dr. Krisellen Maloney was hired as Library Dean.

Like Drexel, UTSA also embraces the power of partnerships. It created the UTSA Libraries Blue Crew, a team of students and public service staff who serve the university student's research needs. Since the inception of this ambassadorship program in 2013, "The Blue Crew initiative is an attempt to give students a visual cue of where they can go to get help," said Carolyn Cunningham, User Experience Librarian (retrieved from http://lib.utsa.edu/news/blue-crew/). "Now, students don't have to differentiate between which staff members to approach," she said.

"I hope students will start to feel comfortable asking anyone with a blue shirt and name tag questions whenever they're in our libraries," Cunningham said, "and over time I hope we can build a reputation as their first stop with any research or assignment questions" (retrieved from http://lib.utsa.edu/news/blue-crew/). The library Web site explains that "Students also have the advantage of asking their own peers for help. The library peer coaches—a group of five student workers trained to help students with library-related inquiries—roam library spaces, making themselves readily available to answer questions." In an article by Stephanie Sanchez, Lius Jasso, an architecture student and peer coach, said "We get a lot of questions about finding books and looking for databases. We just want to make ourselves visible, so students know we're a reliable source." Information can be found at http://lib.utsa.edu/news/blue-crew/.

According to the ALA News section at http://www.ala.org/news/press-releases/2014/04/eight-selected-winners-2014-john-cotton-dana-library-public-relations-award, UTSA library staff "developed this campaign to help the campus improve student retention by making the library staff more accessible to its high-needs student population. The library staff, with its new identity as the Blue Crew, demonstrated its eagerness to hear all student questions through innovative strategies such as collecting questions on blue post-it notes stuck on library display windows (example: 'how much sleep do I really need?')."

Due to the success of the program, the UTSA Libraries also recorded a 48% increase in reference questions in 2013. According to Anne Peters, Director of Communications at UTSA, "By making staff identifiable with their shirts and giving them a brand, we've also elevated the perception of their professionalism and expertise. It's clearer that our staff do much more than just shelve books and check-out items. They're there to assist students with their research and course assignments" (e-mail communication—October 15, 2014).

The UTSA libraries also submitted an application for and were awarded the prestigious John Cotton Dana Award, which is granted by the ALA each year at its annual conference. Peters says at UTSA, "The Blue Crew initiative touched just about every department in the library, directly or indirectly" (e-mail communication—October 15, 2014). She says that, "When we won the

John Cotton Dana, we really emphasized to that it was a result of the efforts of the entire staff—not just the Communications team" (e-mail communication—October 15, 2014). This exemplifies that successful organizations understand the effort to thrive as a twenty-first century library is both team-oriented and staff-initiated. Without the efforts of the entire organization, the best laid out plan will be unsuccessful.

The UTSA summary statement explains that although the libraries were bursting with students before the Blue Team program began, those students were not asking very many questions. In launching its Blue Team, the library retooled and embarked on a yearlong marketing campaign to re-brand their reference services. See http://www.ala.org/news/press-releases/2014/04/eight-selected-winners-2014-john-cotton-dana-library-public-relations-award for more information. Peters commented that "It's fair to say that our students see our staff as more approachable than pre-campaign" (e-mail communication—October 15, 2015).

6.3 POC—Faculty

Collaborations with faculty members can also help improve the library image. Faculty members who have positive impressions of, and experiences with the library are more likely to refer their students to the library to complete classroom assignments. Faculty support and input are necessary because they express their concerns and discuss teaching issues or needs directly with the administration as well. When the administrators understand the library's importance, the administrators help the library by adding to budgets, increasing space, creating new programs and services, as well as eliminating outdated research models, services, or resources. If the library is perceived negatively by the faculty, their support will wane, and libraries then run the risk of snowballing negative opinions. If negativity looms, funding may be impacted. The rate at which students use the library, and the number who are directed to do so by their faculty, are linked to the security of not only the library, but also the librarians' profession. Job security equates to professional security. A handful of savvy librarians is not enough. The information train is leaving the station and librarians can either climb aboard, or be left behind.

Communication is essential to POC. "If librarians truly believe that it is their right and obligation to become partners in the processes of education and scholarship, effective collaboration is essential" (Kotter, 1999, p. 295). "A few extra minutes each day in meaningful conversation with classroom faculty could spell the difference between success and failure" (Kotter, 1999, p. 297). Each discussion provides lessons for librarians who want to improve relations with classroom faculty, he says. In addition to conversational means of gathering data, librarians must also use concrete survey methods. "Without knowing where librarian-faculty relations stand, success in improving these relations is unlikely" (Kotter, 1999, p. 295). "Why not ask each party how they feel about the other? If appropriate surveys can be developed using proven survey methodology, this might resolve the dilemma. In fact, many general user surveys have attempted to assess classroom faculty attitudes or levels of satisfaction"

(p. 296). Remember the data gathered through online surveys, paper surveys, focus groups, and personal interviews are priceless.

According to Yang (2000, p. 128), it's clear that faculty generally want to take advantage of library offerings, "but the first step is educating faculty in the availability of specialized services." If they use the library, then so will their students.

Partnerships between librarians and faculty are also crucial. Because some faculty are not yet acclimated to our broad offerings, especially online searching, we should promote the resources in library instruction sessions, orientation tours, lectures, and faculty council or senate meetings. Some faculty haven't kept up with the technology and may misdirect students in their assignments. For this reason, a collaborative in-service will foster greater connections between faculty and librarians, ultimately benefitting both students and the faculty themselves. Faculty outreach and in-servicing will get faculty involved in many key library programs, such as:

1. Library instruction
2. Faculty council and faculty senate meetings
3. Co-authoring and research services
4. Faculty event planning

Faculty need to understand the benefits of library instruction. Concomitantly, librarians need to understand and provide what the faculty want in a library instruction program. For example, do they want an in-class lecture or demonstration, do they want a library tour, or do they want a workshop environment? The research methods that a marketing team creates will provide that critical data. Additionally, faculty who learn about library instruction will most often become attendees and may even collaborate with librarians on assignments in such sessions.

Faculty and nonfaculty librarians may request a few minutes at faculty council or senate meetings. They can attend administrators' meeting as well. In such meetings, librarians can showcase existing services or changes in services. For example, the librarians can sign up for and provide training in ProQuest Flow, a Web-based citation management system. But without communicating that to the faculty and/or administrators, the services and the resources dedicated to it are absolutely wasted.

In other examples, librarians can ask faculty to partner in collection management, which involves them in weeding, preservation and collection development, and collection evaluation. Academic departments can develop or expand upon library advisory committees. Such committees evaluate collections, make acquisition selections, and create department-wide criteria for library assignments. These assignments can oftentimes benefit from librarian input, and in this way, partnering opens many doors. Finally, consider attending faculty departmental meetings to share the acquisition of new resources or the creation of new programs.

Additionally, in many ways, "faculty in-services teach faulty how they and their students can most effectively conduct research using the library resources and its technology, while utilizing a modern approach" (Lucas, 2011, p. 118). When we promote library services, "we illuminate the reasons why academic libraries are a campus mainstay" (p. 118). The positive experiences that this lends will foster the good word-of-mouth advertising we so covet. "Once you have conducted several in-servicing sessions, faculty will market the services to other faculty members, a method that will drive up the number of in-servicing sessions provided" (Lucas, 2011, p. 119). Schedule the sessions by appointment only, and make "house-calls" whenever possible. Faculty do not want to sit at a public desk for an intense research lesson because it exposes them to students. Faculty are leery of this because it then appears that they are not knowledgeable, and this might affect how their students perceive them and their expertise. Offering "house-calls" creates a special niche for the librarian's in-service program.

When planning a faculty in-servicing model, consider promoting the following:

- Research assistance—encourage the faculty to send students to the research desk for assistance finding resources.
- ILL and document delivery—are students having problems navigating the library resources to find the full-text articles they need? The ILL and document delivery programs will provide what they need, once they know it exists and how to use it. In partnering, librarians communicate with the faculty who also need to use the service in their own professional research.
- Library instruction—what better method of library exposure exists? Library instruction teaches campus students how to evaluate electronic and Web-based resources and select research appropriate for their assignments. In addition, we teach students what they need to use to affectively use the library. The in-service we provide will mirror a library instruction session in that we are helping faculty better understand the library instruction program. In many instances, faculty members are so impressed with the in-service that they immediately realize how beneficial it will be for students to attend a library instruction session. Again, positive experiences breed positive experiences. If the faculty see benefits to instruction then they will tell their students the same thing: the library is a useful and used location of resources, services, and helpful people.
- Online database and Internet searching (Google Scholar, government Web sites, other reputable resources)—In the same way that librarians educate the students, librarians teach faculty how to evaluate online and Web-based research. While some faculty are educated about the usefulness of Google Scholar, for example, others are either resistant or ill-informed as to its benefits and usages. These sessions are the best time to promote what the library does offer, while soliciting what ideas attendees may have regarding improving these offerings.

Online databases are electronic indexes that researchers consult when seeking academic journal articles, newspaper articles, conference proceedings, and other ephemeral periodical materials. These research items are commonly found in a full-text format through library databases. However, in some instances, these articles appear only in abstract or citation-only format. Faculty are aware of this, but they may not understand the next steps in the research process. Faculty can then consult the print collections, other databases, Google Scholar and Google, or then turn to ILL services.

Many faculty who went to colleges and universities prior to 1985, when indexes were still primarily available in print only, are not aware of the ease with which articles can be obtained through online research. Despite this change, which occurred almost 30 years ago, some faculty still create print-resource-based assignments even though by 2010, online databases had almost exclusively replaced print indices.

Marketing online databases accomplishes such goals as educating faculty on how to conduct online research and educating them on the availability of scholarly information online (e.g., Google Scholar, PubMed, and the NIH). Promoting online databases to faculty enables faculty to confidently refer students to online resources that are provided by library subscription. At this point, it is more reasonable to instruct faculty on the difference between scholarly articles and popular magazines, and how their students normally do not understand the exact differences between the two. Imparting this knowledge promotes library resources and it creates a partnership in teaching both the faculty, and if successful, by extension, the students.

Faculty use our resources to conduct professional research and to create library assignments for their students. Marketing online databases and working with the faculty encourages collaboration between faculty and librarians. For example, librarians and faculty can create research assignments in conjunction. As faculty members begin to understand that librarians are truly savvy in the use of online resources, they may be willing to co-write assignments or consult librarians as they create research assignments.

- ILL—tell the faculty that ILL exists for students, and the general campus population, including faculty. If it's a free service, let them know! Give them policy information, turnaround times, overdue fine rates, etc., so they can spread the word to their students. ILL is traditionally a service used by upper-level undergraduates and graduate students so be sure to tell the faculty involved in teaching these types of students. If you use a Web-based interface, such as ILLiad, give a brief demonstration. Smaller libraries more often focus their collections to support their school programs and departmental curriculum. The breadth of the library budget is not able to support infinite research interests. Faculty understand this, and often suppose that smaller colleges have fewer resources. However, library in-servicing provides the perfect chance to promote ILL and create a service partnership with ILL. Explain to the faculty that the in-house collection supports the school curriculum, and that materials supporting a faculty member's specific needs may not be housed within your campus library. In this emerging partnership, you can also encourage faculty to be more proactive in collection management, so that if a resource is needed and they feel their home library should contain these items, then the library becomes informed and makes a potential decision to add them to the collection. Otherwise, they are exposed to the ILL program and its benefit to their research. Collection management—acquisitions, weeding, and preservation. Faculty sometimes need research or instructional materials that the library does not own. Instead of using ILL services, faculty can participate in collection management, including acquisitions, weeding, and preservation. By partnering with faculty, the librarians learn more about what faculty teach, what they research, and what they publish. Partnering with individual faculty helps build a collection that fulfils all these needs. When discovering specialized research interests and trends that are discipline-specific, it becomes possible to partner with faculty by conducting research with them. Co-authoring may be one of the most intense ways to bridge the gap between faculty and librarians, even if the librarians in question have faculty status.

When we demonstrate our competencies in our faculty's disciplines, they gain a better understanding of our work and respect for our libraries. It is a promotional method on par with more expensive and time-consuming efforts. Faculty in-servicing is, after all, free to implement. It only requires staff time.

6.4 POC and administrative or inter- and intradepartmental partnerships

Interdepartmental partnerships are extremely important for positive and efficient public service interactions. Librarian-to-librarian and librarian-to-staff partnerships prove to also be effective methods to improve services that patrons interact with, creating better experiences, which in turn create positive word of mouth. Just as partnering with faculty increases awareness of library services, librarian-to-librarian and librarian-to-staff collaborations increase internal awareness of library services and resources.

In regards to Instant Messaging (IM), consider this: "if a colleague is struggling with a reference question, a discreet IM tip could help her out. In between reference transactions, IM could be used to discuss projects with other librarians" (Atwater-Singer & Sherrill, 2007, p. 48). In other ways, librarian-to-staff interactions can prove meaningful. "One could IM the other departments for the answers without interrupting the reference transaction" (p. 48). For example, if a patron is searching for a newly acquired book, an IM between the research librarian and the acquisitions department can quickly provide the student with the desired resource.

Another example of an effective partnership is a reader's advisory group created to obtain reading materials and spaces. In such a partnership, a research librarian or subject specialist librarian can pair up with the collection development or acquisitions librarian. Maybe they can also involve a facilities manager to locate spaces, or an events coordinator to help promote the advisory group. Working with an events coordinator or campus public relations staff is especially helpful if the library is too small to hire its own communications specialist, as may be more commonly done in university libraries. Additionally, if the library does have a marketing librarian or administrator, this staff member can work with the campus communications specialist for tips, to share vendors, to collaborate on special projects and events. It may even be advisable to team up with the athletics department to create designated study spaces and information literacy classes for at-risk student athletes. Other possible partnerships include service offices, such as a learning center and computer lab or teaming up with residence halls to create "a library in your dorm."

6.4.1 Faculty event planning

It's possible to engage faculty when honoring them for scholarly success. Faculty who have published books and journal articles, or presented at international conferences, demonstrate a high level of expertise and commitment to their research. Published faculty members appreciate being honored by the library for their accomplishments.

Case study: Rutgers University celebration of recently published faculty authors

Rutgers University is located in New Brunswick, New Jersey. The Rutgers University Libraries system consists of 28 libraries, on five campuses, with over 3,709,034 print volumes. In 2014, they reported to have circulated 503,598 volumes in the previous year. In 2014, its large staff consists of 76 librarians, 192 support staff, and 83 student assistants. Rutgers is one of the oldest universities in nation. It was originally chartered in 1776 as an all-male college called the Queen's College, and in 1826 it was renamed Rutgers University. In 2014, they reported to have more than 65,000 students from all 50 states and more than 115 countries.

In 2014, the Rutgers 11th annual publications exhibit opened. Formally titled the *2014 Celebration of Recently Published Faculty Authors*, the library event focuses on displaying recent faculty publications. And it has become a much anticipated and highlighted event. Harry Glazer, the library Communications Director and Chair of the Marketing/Communications Team, says faculty love the event (personal interview, March 31, 2014). In fact, this is an ideal example of libraries as partners in the academic community. By coordinating the event, the library gathers faculty, students and staff from across all campuses to celebrate the accomplishments of their esteemed colleagues. And the faculty can, in turn, see what each other publishes. The university libraries feel that events such as this put them on the map, Glazer says.

RUTGERS
University Libraries

2014 Celebration
of Recently Published
Faculty Authors

EXHIBITION OPENING RECEPTION

Wednesday, March 26, 2014 • 5:00 pm
Archibald S. Alexander Library
The Atrium • Lower Level
169 College Avenue
New Brunswick, NJ 08901

The exhibition will run March 27 – April 30 and will be on display in the lobby of the library.

RUTGERS
University Libraries

2014 Celebration
of Recently Published
Faculty Authors

EXHIBITION OPENING RECEPTION

Wednesday, March 26, 2014 • 5:00 pm
Archibald S. Alexander Library
The Atrium • Lower Level
169 College Avenue
New Brunswick, NJ 08901

The exhibition will run March 27 – April 30 and will be on display in the lobby of the library.

The Libraries eleventh annual Celebration of Recently Published Faculty Authors exhibition and reception honors the recent publications of Rutgers faculty. Executive Vice President for Academic Affairs Richard Edwards and Vice President for Information Services/University Librarian Marianne Gaunt will greet all exhibition participants at the opening reception.

Faculty members are welcome to contribute their recent publications to this exhibition. Publications will be added to the Libraries collections at the conclusion of the exhibition.

Please send books, CDs, and/or DVDs by Friday, March 1st, to: Harry Glazer, Communications Director, Libraries Administration, c/o Alexander Library, 169 College Ave., New Brunswick, College Ave. Campus.

All faculty members and staff are invited to the exhibition opening reception. To RSVP call 848/932-7505 or send email to events@rulmail.rutgers.edu.

RUTGERS
University Libraries

Libraries Administration
Archibald S. Alexander Library
Rutgers, The State University
of New Jersey
169 College Avenue
New Brunswick, NJ 08901-1163

The Libraries eleventh annual Celebration of Recently Published Faculty Authors exhibition and reception honors the recent publications of Rutgers faculty. Executive Vice President for Academic Affairs Richard Edwards and Vice President for Information Services/University Librarian Marianne Gaunt will greet all exhibition participants at the opening reception.

Faculty members are welcome to contribute their recent publications to this exhibition. Publications will be added to the Libraries collections at the conclusion of the exhibition.

Please send books, CDs, and/or DVDs by Friday, March 1st, to: Harry Glazer, Communications Director, Libraries Administration, c/o Alexander Library, 169 College Ave., New Brunswick, College Ave. Campus.

All faculty members and staff are invited to the exhibition opening reception. To RSVP call 848/932-7505 or send email to events@rulmail.rutgers.edu.

RUTGERS
University Libraries

Libraries Administration
Archibald S. Alexander Library
Rutgers, The State University
of New Jersey
169 College Avenue
New Brunswick, NJ 08901-1163

6.5 Community involvement

Library cooperation with the outside community can be both beneficial and creative. It enhances partnerships which directly link to the academic institution mission statement. Jack HangTat Leong says, "community outreach by libraries is the best approach to respond to the increasing significance of community engagement in academic environment." The best library enables interactions between scholars and the general public, he says. "These connections and interactions ultimately lead to the preservation and generation of knowledge and understanding. Available outreach examples are classified into four major categories: (1) community access, (2) information literacy, (3) cooperation, exchange, and partnership, (4) exhibitions and scholarly events" (Leong, 2013, p. 220).

He continues, "An academic library, as a unit of the university that it serves, often defines its mandate according to that of the university. In recent years, the terms 'global impact,' 'knowledge transfer' and 'partner with society' figure prominently among university mission statements (p. 220)."

The ideas he discusses to further this cooperation between the university library and its extra-academic community include partnering on local author book launches, readers advisories, book discussions, seminars, information literacy sessions, panel discussions, conferences, and extending ILL privileges free of charge (if free to the general campus populations). Some benefits of this partnership, Leong says, include building good community relations, or attracting support from an affluent or prominent community group. Furthermore, these relations fulfil the mission of becoming an engaged institution.

Extending information literacy training to young professionals or business leaders in the area is an opportunity for partnerships. It can be difficult to engage those outside the university, so "public libraries and schools, therefore, often partner with academic libraries" to provide this training (p. 224). If we can engage a younger generation in literacy outreach as well, we can help prepare the younger generations for academic success while they attend primary and secondary schools, and continue to support them when they enroll in advanced educational institutions.

As an example, Leong describes events such as "Survivor Day" and "Banned Book Week." These events broaden the offerings that define a library to the general community. Libraries become more that just bricks and mortar, more than just a building of books. It's important for libraries to reach outside of their comfort zones, exploring areas where we can embed ourselves both on campus and off.

Leong concludes that "There are challenges that need to be overcome to make outreach and community engagement work for academic libraries. Common concerns include diversion of limited resources from serving primary user groups, disruption of staff members' routines, and blurring the boundary between academic and public libraries" (p. 230). Concomitantly, "if the academic libraries are providing public access, it may take away the support and resources from public and school libraries" (p. 223). However, he concludes that the benefits of partnering outweigh the concerns, creating a literate and engaged community with the best resources possible, spanning community, and academic libraries.

Schneider (2004) explains "academic libraries determine their interaction with their communities based on three factors: whether a need is expressed from outside the academy, whether they see their mission as an invitation to pursue an action on their own accord, or whether they construct a form of outreach in response to a specific problem or crisis" (p. 199).

An example of a demand for university library resources that initiated outside the campus is the Upward Bound program at D'Youville College. D'Youville is a small independent urban college of approximately 3500 undergraduate, graduate, and doctoral students located in Buffalo, NY. Upward Bound is a local program designed to support academically disadvantaged students who are preparing for a college education. Through the program, these students use the college library one month each summer for study and research http://www.dyc.edu/uwb/. In part, the mission of this small private urban college reads: D'Youville teaches students to contribute to the world community by leading compassionate, productive, and responsible lives.

D'Youville's mission evokes community involvement, so the library has chosen to act on their own accord to further be involved in community partnerships. The D'Youville library also partners with the community by actively participating in a ILL program that borrows from and loans to other schools both locally and nationwide. To specifically partner with local colleges and universities, D'Youville enrolled in an AcademicShare program where students can go to any participating school with their home school identification cards and use the library resources, with some restrictions (http://www.wnylrc.org/index.asp?orgid=394&sid=). It can also be said that these programs arose as a response to a specific problem, because no library can house everything a student might need, therefore resource sharing becomes a necessity.

6.6 Conclusion

Partnerships are collaborative unions between like-minded parties who have mutual interests. Library partnerships will build support from the inside of the building, outward to the general campus. As I previously wrote, "try it and become a library that works to build bridges across campus and boost the usage of their academic library resources and services" (Lucas, 2011, p. 122).

Partnerships are not new to libraries. In fact, in 1880, Winsor wrote, "With the students also the librarian cannot be too close a friend" (Winsor, 1880, p. 9). He is expressing the importance of building partnerships across the campus. We should embrace our contingencies as an opportunity to further our exposure and concomitant importance to the greater college community. "I do not write this as a piece of idealism," he said. "Make the library the grand rendezvous of the college for teacher and pupil alike" (p. 8).

Take advantage of the resources at hand, namely students, faculty, and campus affiliates. As the groups of supporters grow, word spreads, and success follows. By conducting assessments and analyzing data, the library can excel at forming partnerships and creating the buzz of positivity across the community the library serves.

6.7 Discussion questions

1. Discuss the relationship between partnerships and constituents. For example, how might a librarian partner with faculty? How do librarians partner with other librarians and library staff?
2. How can students be recruited as library ambassadors and advocates?
3. Name some potential community partnership events.

References

AcademicShare. http://www.wnylrc.org/index.asp?orgid=394&sid=.
ALA News (2014), Eight selected winners of the 2014 John Cotton Dana Library Public Relations Award. Retrieved at http://www.ala.org/news/press-releases/2014/04/eight-selected-winners-2014-john-cotton-dana-library-public-relations-award.
Atwater-Singer, M., & Sherrill, K. (2007). Social software, Web 2.0, library 2.0, & you: A practical guide for using technology @ your library. *Indiana Libraries*, 26(3), 48–52.
Building great internal partnerships. (2011). In *Business: The ultimate resource*. London, United Kingdom: A&C Black. Retrieved from, http://libproxy2.dyc.edu/login?url=http://search.credoreference.com/content/entry/ultimatebusiness/building_great_internal_partnerships/0.
Bell, C. (2009). Building great internal partnerships. In *Business: The ultimate resource*. London: A&C Black. Retrieved from, http://search.credoreference.com/content/entry/ultimatebusiness/building_great_internal_partnerships/0.
Cassell, K. A., & Hiremath, U. (2013). *Reference and information services. An introduction* (3rd ed.). Chicago: Neal Schuman.
D'Youville College. Upward Bound Program. Retrieved from http://www.dyc.edu/uwb/.
Kilzer, R. (2011). Reference as service, reference as place: A view of reference in the academic library. *The Reference Librarian*, 52, 291–299.
Kotter, W. (1999). Bridging the great divide: Improving relations between librarians and classroom faculty. *The Journal of Academic Librarianship*, 25(4), 294–303.
Leong, J. (2013). Community engagement—Building bridges between university and community by academic libraries in the 21st century. *Libri*, 63(3), 220–231. http://dx.doi.org/10.1515/libri-2013-0017.
Lucas, D. (2011). Faculty in-service: How to boost academic library services. *Collaborative Librarianship*, 3(2), 117–122.
Mathews, B. (2009). *Marketing today's academic library: A bold new approach to communicating with students*. Chicago: American Library Association.
Sanchez, S. (2013). Libraries launch new initiative to reach more students. Retrieved from, http://lib.utsa.edu/news/blue-crew/.
Schneider, T. (2004). Outreach: Why, how and who? Academic libraries and their involvement in the community. *The Reference Librarian*, 39(82), 199–213.
Winsor, J., & Robinson, O. H. (1880). *College libraries as aids to instruction* (No. 1). US Government Printing Office.
Yang, Z. Y. L. (2000). University faculty's perception of a library liaison program: A case study. *The Journal of Academic Librarianship*, 26(2), 124–128.

Resources and services to promote 7

7.1 Market first, promote last

A user-centric approach to developing resources and services will most certainly guarantee that we create what students want. Then we can create successful promotional plans. However, to get there, we must first understand the basic steps to creating our baseline marketing plans. To refresh, *marketing* is the function by which the library keeps in touch with its constituents via constructing sound mission and vision statements, understating SWOT (Strengths, Weaknesses, Opportunities, Threats) analyses, conducting data-driven research and assessments, and creating improvement plans for implementation. *Marketing* also includes revealing, communicating and advertising resources and services, otherwise known as *promotions*. To *promote* is to design educational methods to stimulate constituents' interest in using library resources and services. It involves ongoing activities that strategically reveal and advertise library resources and services. For example, a library should only promote a finite number of new resources at a time. Promoting too many at one time will create information overload and may be counterproductive. Promoting, therefore, should raise the general users' awareness of the library offerings.

Dubicki goes further, stating that promotional methods need to tie the services and resources to their intended audiences. She says that "users associate libraries with books, but few patrons are aware of, or utilize the electronic resources (e-resources)—e-books, e-journals, and databases—that libraries also provide" (p. 6). Instead, she says, most users rely on the general Internet, whether the information gathered this way is accurate or not.

Dubicki also makes this point, and further says that the "promotional message is used to position the library service and establish the brand…promotional materials need to contain a concise, simple message to the benefits which the library products can provide" (p. 11). Many library resources and services may go unnoticed by constituents. Promotions should therefore be tailored to specific user groups. For example, information about resources offered to distance learners should target the distance learners' market base. Focus promotional efforts by devising a means to communicate with those most impacted, linking what libraries offer to who needs or wants to use them.

According to Koontz, "Promotion is only *one* of the important tools of marketing. It's sort of like the index finger is to the human body—it's an essential, strategic part, but still greatly relying on the whole." (Koontz, 2006, p. 4). She says that many libraries create their promotional methods first, without developing a strategic marketing plan. "Promotional tools must be built upon knowledge of your customer markets, their media habits, and the nature of the product or offer" (pp. 4–5).

Marketing is not promotions. Promotions fit into the marketing plan, and should be systematically developed and implemented within project control (see Chapter 5).

7.2 Histories of our leading competition—Easier-to-use resources

Academic libraries have a plethora of resources and services to offer constituents. Libraries can gently guide researchers to better resources than general Internet sites like Google and Wikipedia. Be mindful that librarians must select relevant resources, and offer or design services, and only after conducting their SWOT and constituency assessments—that is, after fully understanding the needs of their researchers and other users. Many resources are available to our general constituencies, and it's important to understand them before we decide to offer them or not. For example, OCLC (Online Computer Library Center) reports that college students feel that search engines and Wikipedia are more convenient, easier, and faster to use than library resources. When combined, 90% of the college student surveyed begin their research using either a search engine or Wikipedia. Absolutely 0% of the students surveyed begin by using the library Web site. How disconcerting. So for all the planning, designing, selecting, analyzing and instruction we offer, nobody consults the library Web site as a starting point. Why is that? If librarians begin to systematically use data derived from SWOT analyses, user assessments, planning, and promoting, we might not be blinded by the light this casts on our professions (see Chapter 9).

Students prefer these new Internet tools and search engines for the ease and convenience they offer. By using such free resources as Wikipedia (Wikipedia.com), Google (google.com), and Google Scholar (scholar.google.com), students access an array of information for use in conducting research and writing papers. These free Internet-based resources are easier to use than subscription based online databases. Perhaps they are more convenient for academic audiences to use than following the process of authenticating to the databases from remote locations. Perhaps we ask our fellow librarians for their opinions and ideas when we should ask the patrons this instead: Why do they Google search when they can library search instead? Students will honestly tell us what they know about the library. We can then assimilate what they acknowledge and fill in the blanks using a data-driven approach.

To understand the challenge these Internet resources present, let's review their history. The beta testing for Google Scholar commenced in October 2004; the service was introduced in November of 2004. The site allows researchers to find scholarly information, mainly in the forms of peer-reviewed journal articles, theses, abstracts, and legal opinions and court cases. The journals of Europe and America also include some nonpeer reviewed articles and scholarly books as well.

Some of the scholarly articles indexed on Google Scholar are freely available in a downloadable full-text format. However, most abstracts connect users to commercial and publisher Web sites, which then require that researchers register and/or pay for a subscription. Many articles are available on a pay-per-view or one-time-only download. Google Scholar continues today to affect interlibrary loan services because many articles that are found on Google Scholar are hosted free online, so the need to use interlibrary loan, pay for requests from other libraries, and wait as the item is shipped, either electronically or physically, is significantly diminished.

Mainstream popular fiction and nonfiction are still mainly searchable at Google. Although it is possible to find full text of many classic books, via resources such as Hathi Trust, it would be difficult for many researchers to find this content without assistance. And as librarians, we have come to learn that Google will generally take us to a site where the book can only be purchased. Libraries could consider convincing Google Scholar to search library online catalogs and provide access links to the home library of each patron. In other words, in a twenty-first century match-up that would actually optimize the benefits of libraries and best serve researchers, if Google Scholar would search library online catalogs, patrons could find the books they need in their own libraries. This would serve a need, as the typical student or researcher does not know how to use WorldCat to find out what books are available in libraries in print or electronic formats. It's not intuitive, convenient or easy to find.

Google Scholar was designed to be a universally used library of scholarly resources. It's a coordinated and central effort that has lived up to its expectations. For researchers, it's easier to use than most resources academic libraries traditionally subscribe to, including such tools as Serials Solutions, Article Linker, and Summon. And no matter how we compare them, none are as intuitive or seamless to use as Google Scholar. By the late 1990s and early 2000s, libraries were subscribing to federated search engines. In an attempt to mimic Google Scholar, "discovery tools" like Ebscohost Discovery Service and Summon were developed by library vendors. Google Scholar may be an unconventional library tool, but its ease of use makes it clearly a winner in the eyes of researchers. Instead focusing on the perception that Google Scholar is better than the library, or outside of our offerings, let's create the perception that it is part of us and part of our offerings. They do not have to be the competition. They can be assimilated. Free or not, Google Scholar is a darn good tool. Although its debut was marred by resistance, librarians over the years have warmed up to the resource. Many, although not all, libraries link to Google and Google Scholar proudly and prominently, advertising this resource as a library offering, instead of a library competitor. Let's turn our competitors into partners.

7.3   Marketing what sets us apart

Unlike Google Scholar, moreover, libraries offer a personal touch. We can see and hear our patrons. When they approach a desk, call on the phone, or text a librarian, a human is reached. We provide personalized service. Of the services we offer, customer service is paramount. With good customer service comes good public relations. This encourages good word of mouth. As we saw in chapter two, John Cotton Dana believed that the best publicity is carried by word of mouth. Libraries also offer physical spaces...spaces by which we actually access the Internet resources. People enter our doors to relax, study, collaborate, surf, discover, and learn. The library, in addition, provides access to tools that the Internet does not loan. We have physical items, tactile in nature. From books, to journals, to laptops, cameras, and audiovisual materials, we offer what the Internet cannot. The library as place is still tangible. When most patrons think of libraries they think of books. According the OCLC Perceptions of Libraries, 2010, 35% of college students say the library's most recognizable role is to provide books, videos, and music. A place to read was listed at 32%. The library is also a physical entity where students can gather, discuss, practice, share, and ultimately learn. We must offer them what they need for success by partnering with other campus entities to provide such services as tutoring, IT support, graduate lounges, comfortable and safe study spaces, and computer word processing stations.

How do we spread the word about the benefits that set us apart? Dubicki says that "once a message for promoting a product is created, a promotional campaign is developed. It is impossible to promote every library service concurrently, so it is important to clearly define the specific objectives of the promotional campaign" (p. 11). She says that successful campaigns are not one-shot deals. Rather, repetition is the key to success. Several methods can be used in the library's promotional campaign. Dubicki lists the following ideas.

- Direct selling—word of mouth
- Print brochures
- Posters
- Giveways
- Open houses
- Workshops
- Research guides
- Newsletters and Web site messages
- Targeted e-mails
- RSS (Rich Site Summary or Really Simple Syndication) feeds
- Course management software
- Social media Advertising, student newspapers, etc.

Promotional campaigns should help the constituents understand what libraries do better than the competition. This will vary from institution to institution. Let's look categorically at the general marketing initiatives that can be taken to create a greater sense of campus constituency enlightenment. Those ideas she presents can be divided into conceptual categories; let's explore them as they relate to promotional campaign inclusion:

- Providing great customer service
- Embedding the librarian into campus life
- Creating new messages using different communication medium

7.4 Customer service

Peer-to-peer testimonials are powerful promotional tools. This is direct selling—creating a word-of-mouth buzz on campus. If the library provides great customer service, students will tell students, and faculty will tell faculty. Great customer rapport can be developed at the research desk, through an efficient interlibrary loan program, and other services, such as circulation, reserves, and multimedia equipment offerings. Additionally, the library can create new data-driven resources or services and expand current offerings, such as providing and promoting citation assistance, tutoring niches, research consultations, laptop loans, and coffee-kiosks.

At Texas A&M, librarians created a "*get it for me*" service. Traditional "*get it for me*" programs are an expansion of Interlibrary Loan programs. Many libraries use this program as an umbrella that includes document delivery, book retrieval services, and book chapter reproductions. Research at Texas A&M University (TAMU) libraries showed that "close to two-thirds (63%) of the respondents found out about the *Get it for me* service from the TAMU library's home page. Word of mouth also played a big role in promoting/advertising this service, from colleagues (17%), friends/classmates (16%), library personnel at the service desk (16%) or library instruction classes/tours (13%)" (pp. 98–99). What the researchers did not point out however, is that when totaled, word-of-mouth promotion runs equal to Website promotion (63% vs. 62%). Word of mouth and good customer service is still key to finding new patrons, creating loyal current patrons, and converting patrons who might favor free non-library supported Web-based resources.

Similarly, OCLC's report found that "college students who have been assisted by a librarian are overwhelmingly (90%) satisfied with their experiences with librarians, and eight out of ten agree that librarians add value to their search process." That is a good testimonial.

7.5 Embedding librarians into campus life

A second set of activities aims at better embedding librarians into campus life. This can be achieved via participation and personal exposure—by attending and hosting special events, like open houses, sporting events, award ceremonies, receptions, and graduation commencements, as well as attending faculty events, councils, and senates. Librarians must seek to become active members in campus life by exposing themselves to the community the library serves. We must be willing to put ourselves out there.

It is good to attend special events and regular gatherings within the community and elsewhere on campus. But also consider what campus activities librarians can create, often in-house: library instruction workshops, readers advisories, poetry readings, Academy Award movie screenings...be creative.

Course management software links provide another opportunity for embedding the library and librarians into students' academic life. These allow us to be present at sites students already visit. When working on assignments, students can easily and quickly navigate from Moodle, for example, to the library online database page or specific required readings.

7.6 Communications

Another category of promotional activities is communications via print materials—creating brochures, branding, and posters. In this area it is preferable to use expert graphic artists. If the library is small, or the librarian working solo, interns or volunteers can help design and produce these communications. Many mid-size libraries can work with a campus publications department to create quality products.

Although messages can be published on the library Web site, keep in mind that this only reaches the library's existing market, this is discussed in greater detail in Chapter 8. Creating and disseminating library newsletters and press-releases to the entire campus community increases exposure. To generate exposure from another campus group, such as human resources, the student association, the residence life committee, or the commuter association, librarians can participate in on-campus interviews. Email messages can also effectively be used for promotions. Consider the impact email has, when OCLC reported 99% of all college students say they use e-mail, daily.

Social networking sites—such as Twitter, Facebook, and Pinterest can place librarians in a position to reach out to constituents in their preferred social spheres. The key to success is knowing the library's boundaries. Not all students want authoritative campus entities, such as a library page, a librarian, or a professor, as Facebook friends. However, partnering with student associations might allow the library to post to these sites without "friending" researchers. For example, the library could post on the Sociology Student Association group page or partner with those types of groups so they can share the library posts (see Chapter 8).

Creating them with some pizzazz helps keep both staff and constituents interested. According to Fisk and Summey, "graphic identity refers to such things as a two-or three-dimensional logo, a slogan, typography, or the use of color" (p. 88). At their home library, they worked with a graphic designer to create a logo, which was then presented on the library Web site, library publications, and brochures. Many items can be created with the library's brand, including pencils, pens, pins, staplers, post-its, book bags, water bottles, book marks, notepads, folders, can cozies, and more. Of all the promotional methods mentioned, librarians most love giveaways. This is by far the easiest part of the marketing process and staff will have many fun ideas to contribute. "Promotional tools must be built upon knowledge of your customer markets, their media habits, and the nature of the product or offer. The message is affected by these important factors. Your customers may be (and likely are) different from any other library's. In short, emulating another library's promotional tools may be risky" (Koontz, 2006, p. 5). Allow the library to create what is in its best interest, what the constituents would respond most positively too. For example, a distance learning college library might spend more time and resources developing a promotional campaign for e-books than a traditional undergraduate campus might. The traditional campus might give in-person training, while the distance education library would need to develop instructional videos to teach their constituencies to use such resources.

In all these efforts, it is important to garner buy in as well. Dubicki stresses that it is essential to keep the library staff informed of the schedule of promotions. Train the trainer, she says, so that "you build confidence and gain strong advocates for the service, and the campaign becomes a more cohesive effort with the participation of all library staff" (p. 13).

7.7 Discussion questions

1. What are the three main categories of promotional methods?
2. What promotional methods are discussed within these categories?
3. What promotional methods would best serve your library and why?

References

Dubicki, E. (2007). Basic marketing and promotion concepts. *The Serials Librarian, 53*(3), 5–15.

Fisk, J., & Summey, T. P. (2005). Got distance services? Marketing remote library services to distance learners. *Internet Reference Services Quarterly, 9*(1–2), 77–91.

Koontz, C. (2006). Promotion is not the same as marketing. *Marketing Library Services: MLS, 20*(1), 3–6, p. 4.

Perceptions of libraries (2010). Context and community: A report to the OCLC Membership.

Using technology to market and promote

8

8.1 Introduction

Think TIPR in regards to analyzing the library's Web site goals. Thinking and investigating always precede planning and reacting. As a specific example, Kiran Kaur's (2009) article "Marketing the Academic Library on the Web" sends a message that marketing can actually effectively be done via the Web. This peer-reviewed article, which passed the litmus test for sound research, is misleading to readers. *Marketing* is planning for the future, as outlined in great detail in Chapter 3. It is an ongoing process of examining what we do, how we do it, what we should strive for in the future, and how we plan to get there. *Promotion* is what happens on the library Web site.

Investigate the library's opportunities and strengths. "We librarians and content managers need to determine the goal of the Web site and then determine the metrics by which Web librarians will measure success" (Whang, 2007, p. 95). In "Measuring success of the academic library Web site using banner advertisements and Web conversion rates: A case study," Michael Whang discusses Hunt and Moran's definition of conversion rates. This is the "ratio of 'lookers' to 'buyers'—how many people come to the sites vs. how many perform an action" on the site (p. 98). That is, how many visitors are converted to regular users? It is ratio of the times that library Web clicks result in actions taken in that regard, for example, the number of library Web site hits versus the number of book renewals when initiated by a Web banner advertising such services.

Think about our current world where all students using Google or Google Scholar are directed back to their home library for full text articles, via library associations linked in the Google scholar preferences. Imagine also, a Google world where the Google Scholar links to the home library resources are seamless and easy. Current discovery tools' links are clunky and confusion reigns; as a specific example, Ebscohost doesn't play nicely with ProQuest, and vice versa. Imagine also search results for books that link researchers to their home library catalog, instead of to Amazon or Barnes and Nobles. If students were directed to their libraries for all book holdings, then we would have effectively marketed and promoted "outside" of our "captive audience."

The phenomenon of promoting to captive audiences may be a relatively recent development. Certainly during the early days of promotions, when libraries used street banners and newspaper announcements (see Chapter 2), they were promoting services to a wider patron base. In todays' society, posting announcements to the library Web site only caters to those actively using that Web site, i.e. the "captive audience." Librarians still have not learned a valuable lesson: we must tap into our hidden market, those who don't know what we do, how we do it, and why we do it. For example, library services aren't truly promoted on the library Web site. We more often just post a Web link to a highlighted program. Programs such as ILL are more often promoted in library instruction sessions, during reference desk transactions, or in faculty in-servicing. These promotions help librarians reach their *visible* market.

It's time to change. Marketing is not promotion, and our visible market is smaller than our hidden market. Promotional methods might involve giveaways of pencils, banners, balloons, etc. But if only our visible market is exposed to our promotions, we are losing ground; we need to expose our resources and services to our hidden market. We learn to access this hidden market through market-based research (see Chapter 3). We access them through developing a sound marketing plan via surveys, interviews and focus groups across the entire campus. Merely listing or announcing new services and resources on a library Web site only hits part of our potential user base: the constituents who already use what we offer. The goal of promotions is to hit a larger percentage of our campus constituents. The *2010 Perceptions of Libraries* report from OCLC says, for example, preparer Gauder wrote that 17% of users say that their library advertises its services. How does the other 83% feel? Do they know what the library does if the library doesn't advertise?

The 2010 OCLC report also stated that:

> *Just 17% of information consumers have seen an advertisement from their library ... Those who were aware of library advertising noted that signs, flyers and promotions inside the library were the most-used methods of advertising. We know that this is not where the information consumer is looking for information.*
>
> p. 98

The report also shows that 77.3% of the US population has Internet access. If we only use the library's Web site or other Internet-based tools to promote, we do not reach that 32.7% of the population. And this is the population most in need of access. How do we reach that unconnected audience?

How can we use technology to reach the hidden market? One idea is to tweet to the entire college community; another is to post comments and links to Facebook pages that belong to larger campus groups. Each social media or Web-based tool used for promotions should be employed with an intention to create a new partnership beneficial to both parties.

Socially, where do academic libraries fit in? How does our mission support the social needs of our campus constituents? While many libraries do host special functions or events that are social in essence, how do we promote these events? Social media has become a common tool for libraries, but our skills in such media may be hit or miss. Do we or don't we reach our intended audiences, and if so, how do we create the phenomenon that so many other social media "posts" enjoy? Creating a buzz is, after all, the intended result. We want people to use and to enjoy our messages, videos and pictures. How do we accomplish this? One way is to get other campus constituencies to provide links to the library from their Web sites. The library Web site is more of a tool to be used for gathering the data needed to analyze statistics regarding who uses what or the number of hits on the Pharmacy Subject Guide vs. the Chemistry subject guide, for example. The only benefit to promoting resources and services on the library Web site is to encourage our visible market to become more loyal partners and advocates.

8.2 Social medium

Marketing has become a two-way street. Once, the marketing messages were initiated and controlled by the business or service owner. Today, through social media, customers, and more importantly to us, campus constituents, have the ability and interest in discussing, reviewing, tweeting, and posting information about a service or product. Broken down, this equates to more than letting the buyer beware. It also means, let the producer beware. What we say, do, offer, post, create and maintain is subject to mass scrutiny or praise. And let us prepare for the worst, while striving to obtain the best in service quality.

"Social networks are the actually virtual communities that are generally found over the Web where members of common purposes or interest share an unlimited and unrestricted amount of information" (Yazdanifard, Obeidy, Yusoff, & Babaei, 2011, p. 578). Therefore, social networks are a means to reach captive audiences. However, due to the nature of social networks, and the theory of Six Degrees of Separation, constituents may be exposed to social medial promotions, and hidden audiences may be reached via library-related messages through friends' or colleagues' social media feeds, such as Facebook posts, Twitter feeds and YouTube videos, all shared over the Internet.

"Social sharing, whether online through social media or peer-to-peer communication, assures recipients that the information is worth their time—since it comes from a trusted source, friend, or colleague. Social endorsement is essential to the accelerated spread of viral information. As the information is shared among peer groups, the number of recipients increases exponentially" (Thomas, 2011, p. 64). Information shared by friends may gain greater acceptance.

Libraries most often use Internet channels to post surveys, twitter feeds, links to Facebook pages and to other social media sites. Additionally, libraries also use the Internet to announce events or highlight new services or resources. To be most effective, we must look beyond our own Web site for these purposes.

Even though library literature often times mistakes marketing for promotion, as mentioned, valuable wisdom can still be gleaned through these discussions. For example, Kaur reminds us that "the traditional notion of 'librarians know best' has been challenged by the increasing availability of information on the Internet and the World Wide Web" (2009, p. 454).

Unfortunately, he goes on to describe how to do exactly more of what we have always done. At this point in the profession, we all are aware of the threat posed by the Web. We can ask, if our patrons are in fact turning to the Internet, are they doing so at the beginning, middle or end of the research process? And if we focus on what Kaur calls "marketing the academic library on the web" how many potential patrons do we in fact reach? How many of our non-users do we miss? All of them, I suggest. He goes on to ask, "what good are library resources and services if they are not known by the academic community, especially in the web environment…new and innovative methods of publicity are necessary to reach out to these new breed of online users" (p. 457). He sees the need to promote, but doing so on the library Web site only reaches our current users, and fails to capture the attention of the entire academic community.

Additional to the dilemma of reaching only our captive audience, we need to envision methods by which the library Web site is a more useful tool for gathering data and analyzing statistics regarding who uses what; for example, how many times do students use the Pharmacy Subject Guide, or hit the ILL page, only to leave seconds later? Do we also not promote key services such as ILL as well on the library Web site as we do at the research desk, faculty in-services, or in library instruction sessions? This information has to reach our invisible market.

8.3 Twitter

There are two main functions of using Twitter in promoting library offerings. First, it allows us to post information on new programs, services, acquisitions, and events. However, it is also a powerful tool for gathering data about user perceptions and experiences. This is free, unsolicited feedback. That feedback can factor into your marketing plan as well as your promotional efforts. In other words, Tweets can factor into the interpretative phase of TIPR, as it generates qualitative data in the form of free text comments, which may also generate themes and action items. In fact, library guru Stephen Bell suggests that we focus more time on what users say to you and about you (2012).

Once you start tweeting, as a promotional and marketing tool, remain committed to it just as you are to all other communications methods. Active Tweeting then becomes as important as remaining current and active with your Facebook and Instagram posts, likes, shares, etc. Keeping up-to-date and active with Tweets is as important also, as keeping your library website current with information and announcements.

According to Sump-Crethbar, "a library's Twitter feed needs to build relationships, grab people's attention, fit the user's needs, and generate a conversation between the users and the library" (2012, p. 350). She continues to say that media dashboards can help distribute the work among staff. Especially in small organizations, where staff resources are limited, a dashboard will help centralize your social media promotional methods.

8.4 Pinterest

Thornton (2012, p. 164) surveys the current presence of academic libraries on Pinterest and highlights best practices for pinning activities. She also suggests methods of creating profiles, virtual pin-boards, and pinning strategies. Thornton says that "before embarking on the newest online social networking trends, academic libraries should carefully consider the relevance of new technologies for their needs and plan a strategy for mounting a presence."

Pinterest launched in 2010; its founder's goals were to allow registered users to post and share their favorite images, as a modern-day equivalent to photo albums and scrapbooking. Other social media platforms, such as Flicker, Facebook, Twitter, and Snapchat, can also be used to share photos, but none of these is specifically useful for gathering Internet images. "Pinterest allows users ("pinners") to upload images, capture images from the Internet, and re-pin images posted by others to create topic-themed virtual pin-boards," Thornton says (p. 165).

"Libraries can draw visitors to collections, resources, and digitized archival materials, and share information and knowledge. Pin-boards also can be used to market library services and promote library events. Some libraries are already taking tentative steps to embrace Pinterest as a new tool for connecting with users" (p. 165).

Thornton compiled a list of American academic libraries on Pinterest, and found 57 active libraries. Her examination lead to the development of tips and best practice guidelines for using Pinterest. Her most compelling findings include

1. Have clear goals, including a defined plan of action for the profile and the content:
   - 39% of the libraries, for example "failed to display the complete library name."
   - 91% failed to link their library to the respective college or university.
2. Familiarize the library's Pinterest staff with copyright rules. Pinterest does have a "no pin" code so that it is possible to protect images from being re-pinned.
3. Keep content interesting and up to date. "It can also help to publicize local events and share photos of past events" (p. 173).
4. Link images of resources to the library catalog or to resource location for direct access. For example, if pinning an image of a book cover, link that to the library catalog so patrons can find the book and check it out.

8.5 Online games

The library's online gaming initiatives should begin with an end result in mind. Games can be used to teach, to inspire, to coordinate or even to entertain. "In late 2007, the librarians at the University of Alabama (UA) began serious research into building an information literacy game. This effort was born from the library administration's interest in researching library game development after encountering a number of grant opportunities focused on academic games" (Battles, Glen, & Shedd, 2011, p. 115.) Challenges abound, but the authors say, "That does not mean library instruction games are doomed to fail because they can never compete financially with (Call of Duty or World of War Craft), but it does mean a unique approach is needed that allows for the creation of an engaging experience without the game appearing vastly inferior to those commercial products" (p. 116). It's reasonable to create online games that instruct students in using library resources. One example is to create a virtual treasure hunt.

8.6 Library Web sites

According to Connell (2008), "a library Web site is an integral part of a library's identity. Many captive audience patrons visit a library's virtual location, its Web site, more than they visit its physical location" (p. 121). Her research shows that larger schools do not have more resources or advanced technology when it comes to Web page design. Connell's literature review showed that Web design teams are most often comprised of one person (49.0%) followed by two to three members at 28.6%. She says that "since academic library websites are such an integral part of their libraries, it is important to know more about the people, tools, and methods used to create these websites" (p. 121). Additionally, it may be unreasonable to expect that one person can design the site alone. It should be a joint effort that brings together librarians from various departments, who have different training, skills, and experiences working with the patron base.

Additionally, general library literature research shows that most often, librarians themselves are in charge of the library Web site design and team management, and many are self-taught. "Almost half of the libraries surveyed had only one person to do Web design, and the majority of Web designers managed Web work in conjunction with other responsibilities" (Connell, p. 129). Web design is often conducted by librarians who are interested in the work, not necessarily those most skilled in Web design or maintenance. The theory that librarians tend to subscribe to is to avoid having people cajoled to join a team they have no interest serving on. Just because a librarian prefers not to participate should not automatically exclude them. Library supervisors need to step up and do their job of assigning work to their workers.

"Library websites are essential… they're the public face of the institution" (Chow, Bridges, & Commander, 2014, p. 253); our Web sites, they say, have seconds to convince users that what they need is available. Web sites are quickly scanned for answers. With the complexity of the resources the libraries offers, users may be exposed to too much too fast, with scant ability to understand the steps they will need to follow to find information.

Though it most effectively reaches only our current users, the library Web site is still a good way to disseminate targeted Web-based messages. Indeed, this might be one of the most currently used methods to promote library services and resources. "Many libraries now use the Internet to promote their services…they have to compete with everything else on the Web. Library Webmasters must learn the latest techniques in web design in order to make distinct Web sites, and learn how to promote their Web sites in order to get prospective users," (Wenhong, 2006, p. 341). However, as stated, Web sites hit our existing market, whether or not they have ever set foot into the physical library spaces. In fact remote users are as important as physical users. For all the caveats, the Web site is still a critical tool for advertising what is new, old, or interesting.

Let's analyze further. Perhaps our library Web pages are not as easy to use as we imagine. They must be visible, useful and usable, which is similar to the premise by Ranganathan's principle that books are to be used and useful. So too must websites. In this context, at its most base level, we must create pages that can be easily read by patrons. Does the institution have many foreign or TESOL students? Even more basically, are Web site fonts and sizes sufficient so that users of a variety of ages and visual abilities are able to read the content? Additionally, all sites should be free of library jargon, such as "online databases," "library catalog," also avoiding such abbreviations as "circ" for circulation, or "ILL" for interlibrary loan. Chow et al.'s (2014) nationwide

Using technology to market and promote 81

study shows that many library features that seem highly desirable are overwhelmingly lacking in academic Web sites. Among the most notable are the date the library site was last updated (only 19.6% of libraries reported such), the ability to resize text (only 2.0% report such) and spelling out abbreviations or explaining them (8.8% reporting such). Interestingly enough, libraries feel approximately 50% of the time that headings, titles and links are jargon free. These writers show that "usability testing was not a high priority for most library Web sites as 72% reported that they did not conduct usability testing when designing their current website" (p. 261). According to Whang:

> Employing e-metrics as a managerial tool to measure the Web site's success will provide library Web and marketing committees with timely data to help them evaluate their short-and-long term efforts as well as respond quickly to changing market forces and to the needs of [their] consumer-driven constituents. This will help the academic library plan for the future and become a responsive and flexible 21st century library dedicated to supporting the teaching, learning, and research priorities of the institution.
>
> 2007, p. 106

Findings from usability and accessibility studies should help librarians address such questions as: if students cannot find an answer to their questions, will they return? Did students tend to persist until they eventually found answers? And most importantly, if the information is not found, will a student ever return to the library Web site? These usability studies can be incorporated into the marketing plan assessment phase (see Chapter 3).

8.7 Web sites vs mobile apps

The mobile revolution has already started. Brendan Ryan (2011) states that "mobile devices are becoming a fixture of contemporary life" (pg. 128). OCLC reports that in 2005, two-thirds of the American population owned a cell phone. "Today, that number stands at 93%" (2010, p. 13). Ryan finds that many academic libraries are focusing on projects to develop sites that are optimized for mobile devices.

To best design a mobile-optimized Web site, it is important to clearly define the goals of the mobile versus PC or desktop site. What information does the library want users to find? What is the easiest way for users to obtain that data? How many clicks does the team feel is appropriate and navigable?

Chow et al. find that (p. 253) library Web sites consistently provide access to the following information:

- Hours of operation
- Library addresses and contact information
- News and events
- Library catalogs
- Online book renewals
- Feedback sections

These authors say, "users quickly scan a Web site to determine whether they have what they need: Can this site answer my question?" (p. 253). The challenge for libraries is to design the site so it is easy to navigate. The mobile-ready Web site may be the wave of the twenty-first century future in libraries. If libraries consistently provide access to the above-referenced information, why not design both Web presences in the same manner? If users can in fact quickly identify this information on the library's PC Web site, a mobile app that is significantly different may cause transferal confusion. Let's say one site loads with the needed information, while the other encapsulates it into sections, perhaps providing easy-to-navigate protocols. These differences can be resolved. Ask also: if the site has the answer to patrons' questions, can these answers be found easily and quickly, as on Google or Google Scholar, or must patrons employ "hunt and peck" tactical maneuvers?

Library Web sites need to exhibit true ease in usability, not for the librarian (librarian-centric) but for the library patron (user-centric). This echoes *Ranaganthan's Five Rules*: books are to be used and useful. Not much has changed, and we should keep that in mind. Similarly, Web sites should be used and useful. His laws are:

1. Books are for use.
2. Every reader his [or her] book.
3. Every book its reader.
4. Save the time of the reader.
5. The library is a growing organism.

How can a Web site be used and useful if it is not user-friendly? If the site is unnavigable, patrons will not return, so they will not see the library's new program banner, event schedule, newly acquired books, or procedural changes. Again, we lose ground in struggling to keep our captive audience. And losing them is what happens, unfortunately, on a routine basis in academe. As previously mentioned, why not switch to Google Scholar? In all fairness, it's considerably easier than using a discovery tool powered by Ebscohost that does not like to work with its competitor, ProQuest. Such an unfortunate situation. Connell found that only 46.8% of the academic libraries she surveyed conduct usability testing. We need to do this to make our Web sites more competitive. We have the information, and we offer a better service than our Web search competitors—we need to bring these facets of our libraries to our current and potential users.

8.8 Facebook

Partnering can happen with more than just people. Think of how librarians and libraries can create partnerships using the social phenomenon of Facebook. Facebook has created and rekindled friendships across the globe.

According to Phillips (2011), "if Facebook can help cultivate a brand that expands beyond books, students may discover that their library is more relevant and approachable than they previously perceived, and a valuable part of their personal networks" (p. 512). Her research concluded that three domains for partnerships emerged: the library; the library and students combined; and the library in combination with the university, local community, and the broader society. Each participant in the domain benefits from these developing relationships. Her literature reviews show users' mixed reviews of libraries, from those who embrace to those who question its existence in the academic world.

Facebook members ask, what do I like and what do my friends like? A library Facebook page should be rife with likes, comments, posts, pokes and the like—but rarely do we see such activity on a library site. Philips' research included studying the Facebook pages of 30 libraries in the Consortium of Academic and Research libraries in Illinois (CARLI). Of the 30, 25 had Facebook pages. Of those, 17 were considered viable for her research, which showed that "13 of the 17 Facebook pages promote their libraries and/or libraries in general, with promotional messages representing 10% of all posts" (p. 516). We can use our Facebook pages more effectively. Philip suggests that announcement messages include (pp. 515–516):

- Hours of operation
- Service availability
- Facilities (library as place)
- Library policies
- Print or online collection highlights
- Information resources
- Instructional sessions
- Other events
- Other library services
- Requests for feedback

Other post ideas include pictures of student workers interacting with resources, services, and staff. We can initiate a system for making public service announcements, or provide links to YouTube videos or tutorials. Philips says that "it appears that librarians are using Facebook to present themselves as approachable, in order to develop a rapport with students, which could ultimately facilitate the delivery of service" (p. 520). Again, how do we expand our Facebook posts outside of our captive audience, our existing friends, so that we can further our reach? Consider asking related Facebook pages to "share" your posts. For example, if the library announces that it has subscribed to PsychNet on Facebook, it would be helpful to expand reach by asking the Psychology Club or the Psychology Department to "share" the post. Keep in mind your patron base. How many of your constituents are Facebook users? It's not the most popular social medium in the undergraduate age group.

8.9 Discussion questions

1. Name three social networking media that can be used to promote library offerings.
2. Which social networking media are the most available to students?
3. As reported by OCLC, how many Americans owned a smart phone in 2010, compared to 2007?
4. Define marketing. Define promotions.

References

Battles, J., Glenn, V., & Shedd, L. (2011). Rethinking the library game: Creating an alternate reality with social media. *Journal of Web Librarianship*, 5(2), 114–131.

Bell, S. (2012). Students tweet the darndest things about your library-and why you need to listen. *Reference Services Review*, 40(2), 217–220.

Chow, A. S., Bridges, M., & Commander, P. (2014). The design and usability of US academic and public libraries. *Reference and User Services Quarterly*, 53(3), 265.

Connell, R. S. (2008). Survey of web developers in academic libraries. *Journal of Academic Librarianship*, 34(2), 121–129.

Gauder, B. (2011). Perceptions of libraries, 2010: Context and community. A report to the OCLC membership. *OCLC Online Computer Library Center, Inc.*

Kaur, K. (2009). Marketing the academic library on the web. *Library Management*, 30(6/7), 454–468.

Phillips, N. K. (2011). Academic library use of Facebook: Building relationships with students. *The Journal of Academic Librarianship*, 37(6), 512–522.

Ryan, B. (2011). Developing library websites optimized for mobile devices. *The Reference Librarian*, 58, 128–135.

Sump-Crethar, A. N. (2012). Making the most of Twitter. *The Reference Librarian*, 53(4), 349–354.

Thomas, L. C. (2011). Design a double rainbow. *Journal of Web Librarianship*, 5(1), 63–67.

Thornton, E. (2012). Is your academic library pinning? Academic libraries and Pinterest. *Journal of Web Librarianship*, 6(3), 164–175.

Wenhong, J. (2006). Marketing practices in the LCAS. *Library Management*, 27(6/7), 336–343, 341.

Whang, M. (2007). Measuring the success of the academic library Website using banner advertisements and Web conversion rates: A case study. *Journal of Web Librarianship*, 1(1), 93–108.

Yazdanifard, R., Obeidy, W. K., Yusoff, W. F. W., & Babaei, H. R. (2011). Social networks and microblogging: Thebe emerging marketing trends and tools of the twenty-first century. In *The Proceedings of 2011 International Conference on Computer Communication and Management Vol. 5* (pp. 577–581).

Marketing a profession: Marketing the future 9

9.1 Introduction

In 2005, Wysock from the Wall Street Journal reported that professors at a Drexel University campus forum in May of 2005 complained about funding cuts at the library. President Constantine Papadakis did not apologize for the belt-tightening. Papadakis told them he'd prefer to have an all-digital library with no books at all.

Some faculty members and students were concerned. An architecture professor said print is essential to students and scholars in that field. Another professor compared the future Drexel library to that of a community college, saying that it was impossible for a university president to propose a bookless library. Dr. Papadakis says he was overstating. Spending too heavily on books, periodicals, and the buildings that house them is a waste in the digital era, Papadakis said. The discussion regarding marketing libraries and librarians has never been of greater importance. If the largest and most prestigious of universities is considering the demise of a library's print collection and as a physical space, so too will other institutions, until the academic library becomes extinct.

9.2 The time is now. Marketing the profession: If we wait it will be too late

The typewriter was first conceptualized in 1714 by Henry Mill, an Englishman who filed a patent for his idea. However, the first typewriter, as we know it, emerged in 1808, designed by the Italian Pellegrino Turry for his blind friend.

The Sholes and Glidden typewriter appeared in America in 1874, almost 100 years prior to the information explosion in late twentieth century. Let's consider the effective death of the once innovative typewriter. The QWERTY keyboard survived, but it transferred to the electronic world of personal computing, via Windows or Mac. Typewriters themselves are relics: almost extinct. The PC and Mac, successive revolutionary devices, increased exponentially the speed by which the written word can be created and disseminated.

This is only one early twentieth century invention that sparked an information age. Well, librarians adapted to computers, and even thrived as increased in-house efficiencies resulted in better and more innovative services. The next generation of revolutionary devices included the smart phone, tablets, and smart-boards. Information from Google, Google Scholar, Facebook, Twitter, and other sources opened up the flow of information to speeds our ancestors would never comprehend. And in a librarian's imagination exists hope for hologram-like library computer banks, which co-exist along side interactive library spaces that house after-school care programs, discussion groups, political functions, and banquets. The twenty-first century librarian must be imaginative and participate in discussions. This is the future of the profession. How will librarians of the twenty-first century adapt? What will they become? Let's review ways we have survived in the past to guide us to our sustained existence, thriving as the core of academic institutions, as their heart, mind, and spirit.

9.3 Future of marketing libraries and the profession—If we wait, it will be too late

The most recent threat to the profession could be Helpouts by Google. The Google About Helpouts section describes this service as providing live video-based help anytime from experts. Of the experts Google lists, librarians are blatantly left out. "Experts," it says, includes teachers, counselors, doctors, personal trainers, enthusiasts, and more. Where are we in this equation? And why is Google leading the charge?

There are several productive means by which we can promote our own profession, but to do so without developing a marketing plan will only sell us short and, in the end, be counterproductive. We can no longer rely on promotional gimmicks alone. We know the time to market ourselves is now, and we need to understand our own profession well enough to transfer the respect we have for our own to the general academic community and furthermore to society in general.

How will we market our profession? Think TIPR. The past chapters discussed the importance of thinking, investigate, planning, and reacting. This applies equally to the marketing plan for our profession as a whole. This chapter deals specifically with this roadmap. To *think* is to work on our mission, where we are, and our vision, where we want to be; to think about our past, our present, and our future. *Investigate* involves our data assessments, in which we uncover what our patrons and the general community think we do, versus what we do. In this research, one may gather a better understanding of what the community actually wants us to do. Librarians should *plan* a course of action, before *reacting*. In other words, do not skip steps of the process and move directly to promotions. Understand the data first. Form partnerships, determine which resources or services to create, and improve, then promote. Ask, what technologies can we use? Become engaged with the external constituents, the community, as well as with the internal constituents, the librarians. We are customers of one another. We need to TIPR together. Think, Investigate, Plan, React.

The continuity of the profession and perhaps ultimately the existence of academic libraries rely on how well librarians educate our consumers about what we offer to students' academic lives. If we librarians develop a professional image, we will be taken seriously. Librarians need to heed the warning signs. Academic libraries are not safe from downsizing, staff eliminations, or shrinking budgets. If librarians wait, it will be too late.

Due to the explosion in technology, the Internet allows access to an unending supply of information. Many researchers turn to Google to not only begin the research process, but also to end it as well. Librarians face a rise in unmitigated research transactions in the academic environment. If we don't market the librarian as the information provider on campus, the community will never understand why they need such expertise. If patrons do not interact with a skilled librarian, then many will never value the library and the librarian as integral to their academic lives.

To begin, let's examine what we do well. Then we will discuss how to create a professional marketing plan for the profession. Here are concepts to examine:

- Customer service is a librarian specialty. It's our niche. It's what sets us apart from other information generators, including such services as Google Helpouts and Google Scholar.
- Develop partnerships across campus.
- Get involved in campus leadership activities. Outreach by developing the librarian's role on campus. Consider co-publishing with faculty, for example.
- Create a modern professional definition of our role developed through a SWOT analysis, incorporating a mission statement and a vision statement.
- Librarians need to gather data regarding our current professional image on our individual campuses.
- Create and implement the marketing plan. The plan librarians construct should begin using the same steps employed when creating a marketing plan for the library.

According to Debbi Smith in *Strategic Marketing of Library Resources and Services: College and Undergraduate Libraries*,

> "Whether physical or virtual, an academic library's collection and services are relevant only to the extent that they are used by their intended audiences. Use of collection and services is not only a reflection of how well they have been developed to meet the mission and vision of the parent university, the academic curriculum, and faculty research needs. It is also a result of how well-informed the community is about specific resources offered by the library. Our profession is in constant flux as resources continue to move from traditional physical formats to online counterparts and as librarians mediate access to rather than provide ownership of a resource. The profession has had to adjust to libraries no longer being the only information game in town with a captive audience; we face competition from resources that are easily accessed online without our assistance through Google and other search engines or Web sites." (2011, p. 333).

Not only has access to information exploded, so have the ways we communicate. In the past, we only had to worry about who we need to reach, how to reach them, and what to say (Mathews, 2009). There were limited venues for such communications. In marketing the library of today, we have far greater resources at our disposal. Media has exploded in our twenty-first century information age. Now we have to decide what messages to send to which user groups using a multitude of communications methods. Although traditional print and media messages via TV, radio, campus billboards, and effective signage are still useful, we must also now transmit promotional messages via online methods:

- Facebook
- Twitter

- Library generated user Web sites
- Course software, etc.
- Mobile-enabled Web sites
- QRC codes
- Texting
- Virtual reference and chat services

9.4 Customer service

Librarians know that patrons enjoy many benefits from using library resources. When patrons use the services, librarians can easily demonstrate their advantage over the Internet. We provide outstanding customer services to patrons, in ways that the Internet cannot. If a patron has a question of a library resources, data bit, or origin, they can find help at the library. If they have a Google question, experience technical issues, or just don't understand what they are reading, they can call a librarian. Google representatives do not generally assist their users with technical, interpretational, or access related questions. However, Google Helpouts may be a competitor. Helpouts currently offers point of need assist to the user. It is currently the bigger threat to our profession (SWOT).

In "Reflections on Ranganathan's Five Laws of Library science," Leiter (2003) said that people who have reflected on these laws or who are just now reading them "will have their interest rekindled and, in the process, have their professional enthusiasm and inspiration rejuvenated as well" (p. 412). He continues to say that if we lose focus on our profession customer service skills, we will also lose enthusiasm, creativity, and our "professional soul" (p. 412). "Our professional orientation is toward service—always—and as we strive for (and often achieve) excellence in service, it is not surprising that we are taken for granted!" (p. 412).

Customer service is key to the future of academic libraries, and, therefore, the future of academic librarianship. What sets us apart from other organizations is customer service. Patrons want answers. When they work with a librarian, they see librarians verify answers, check sources, and explain results. They expect the same from Google. They do not often understand, again, the higher level of customer service they receive at the library. Whereas Google retrieves results, a librarians retrieves, interprets, and organizes information. We construct, instruct, and deconstruct. Patrons who go to Google and type in a search term do not expect Google to explain how the information was generated. They only expect good results. If we can impart the importance of data verification to patrons, they will learn to question their results in the spirit of intellectual inquisition. Information literacy is our catch phrase, but without the interaction between librarian and patron, the analysis might be forgotten. The patron might assume all information to be correct.

Customer service makes our profession unique in the information age. It is our "gig." Let's promote that! In "The Visible Librarian: Asserting your value with marketing and advocacy," author Siess (2003) says, "Our customers have choices in the acquisition of information and the library or information center may not the first choice" (p. 3). Our potential library constituents might not know why librarians exist or what we do. Therefore they don't know why they need us. The Internet has it all, they believe, and these user groups can simply choose to *completely* ignore us.

It's the people who staff the library who make the library experience memorable. Stephen Abram (1996, p. 4) said "the marketing activity of delivering effective information while highlighting our personal qualities and professional attitudes is key to promoting ourselves." Pave the way with good customer service—wrap up a transaction by giving a patron a memorable experience. The library experience should be all about the patron. Providing this level of service will promote positivity for our profession. Library service is all about what the patron needs, wants, and uses. We should develop a better understanding of this and emphasize this, instead of investing our energies trying to promote random, untargeted or not completely thought out offerings. We cannot expect patrons to use what we offer if it is not in fact what they want or need, just because the services exist.

Perhaps an even more egregious offense is providing poor service. When student complain to their professors that, "My interlibrary loan articles never arrive in time," or "The library never has the books I need," we need to take heed. If they say "I can never find anyone to help me," it's time to evaluate what we do. The preceding comments are significant barriers to improving the image of the library. If the comments can be overheard in the cafeterias and professors' offices across college campuses nationwide, then our profession will suffer. When the profession suffers so do the libraries. Librarians need to be a part of this conversation, rectifying unease, and gaining a better understanding of our student issues. That is customer service.

Customer service is a promotional method, just like giving away free pencils. It is a conscious effort that we make to enhance our image on campus. Give good service and the word will spread from one library patron to another, and from one library user to a nonuser! Customers tend to varying degrees of satisfaction. While some sing our praises, some will never be satisfied, no matter what we do. If the very satisfied and the very unsatisfied are the outlying user groups, then direct efforts toward the middle of the road patrons.

Delivering good customer service affects our library users and nonusers alike. We have potential customers: those who really have not yet used our resources or services. How we serve them is different from how we serve our user base. The problem is, when they initially present themselves, we don't recognize them as belonging in one group or the other. We must strive to provide the best possible service to each customer, regardless of user status. Remember, when we interact with patrons, we can't be certain which group they fall into. Is this a new user, one who was just before considered a nonuser? When we reach out to users, we can ask their status. Have they used a database before, checked out a book before, etc? For examples, we can poll them individually as they approach. Ask "have you…"

- used the library before to…
- checked out a book
- used a database
- gotten the full text of an article
- printed a paper, etc.

Ask a question that helps gage their status, so to better customize their experience. List several of the services students most often use. Then ask the harder questions, the customer-service questions, like: Have you interacted with an ILL staff member/consulted with a librarian/attended a research skills class? Just asking these questions helps deliver a more meaningful experience for the students, the faculty, and the librarian providing the service.

Try to understand the patron's preferences. Many do not know how to find a book in the stacks, but most times, we never even bother to ask. Let's examine an example experience and a barrier to good customer service. If customers attempt to access full text from a library database, can they retrieve it unmitigated, or do they need to interact with a person? Do they know that librarians encourage students to seek assistance from library staff? We run the risk of students engaging in unmitigated interactions, resulting in resources not connecting properly, or not seeming available; in these cases, a student may become confused, give up, use a Web page answer instead, and perhaps fail a paper for using the wrong kind of resource. It is not good customer service to tell a student that what he or she wants is available—effectively, it is not if it is too hard to find on a platform that users feel should be an unmitigated service model. Library resources should be more intuitive to use!

If it is primarily those who staff the library who can make the library experience positively memorable, then library staff have to provide the best service each and every time a patron is served. This includes the unmitigated transactions where the patron uses the services, even if there is little interpersonal contact between the patron and the librarian. Librarians in the past navigated physical library stacks and resources to provide answers, research articles, facts, and information leads. Now the Internet can easily remove librarians from the positive library experience. We have come to develop library tools that mimic the ease of the Internet, for example discovery tools and mobile-enabled Web sites. And we assume students will use them and like them. Do they? Is it easy to do? Have we taken ourselves out of the equation to the extent that students don't even contemplate whether librarians have any special consultative skills to offer them? We need to promote ourselves.

9.5 Mission, vision, and SWOT analysis (Think)

Self-promotion does not equal self-glorification. It isn't even entirely about self-preservation. This is about preserving the profession by creating an awareness of how we work, how we are managed, and how librarians and libraries will grow to better meet users' needs in the twenty-first century.

To market the profession, we must follow the same process we follow in marketing the library. It begins with writing a mission and a vision statement. Marketing the profession also involves understanding our SWOT. It involves creating a plan of action, and it needs to be a universally accepted plan, one that the profession accepts and supports. Who then leads this charge? The librarians of today can direct the way, protecting future librarians. The librarians of today can write the mission, the vision, the SWOT, and then seek institutional support, to implement and then to rally increased professional esteem nationwide; indeed, worldwide. Since all libraries and librarians are different, let's begin on a smaller scale, marketing our libraries and then our profession to our academic constituents. The marketing plan can be customized by individual libraries and librarians, to reflect the unique mission each serves and the unique services each offers.

To contemplate the mission of a librarian we must first open discussions regarding what we do in the twenty-first century library. A librarian teaches information literacy skills. We assist researchers as they sift through a myriad of information. We categorize information. We design information retrieval methods. We classify data. We design research methods. Our vision is being redefined at the moment. In October, 2013, the American Library Association received a grant to create the Center for the Future of Libraries. See http://www.ala.org/transforminglibraries/future for more information.

9.6 Assessment and planning (TIPR: Investigate and plan)

Always assess before planning. Improve the image of both librarians and libraries through the marketing plan: that is the charge of the marketing team. As such, the project control principles can be used to select a team, define the goals, bring on supporters, and schedule tasks and deadline dates. Follow the same steps discussed within this text regarding the library's marketing plan. In doing so, focus on the data. Be sure to conduct literature reviews, surveys, focus groups, and individual interviews. Data leads to effective action. In creating the marketing plan for the profession, let's not forget to promote!

9.7 Form partnerships (TIPR: React)

Librarians can create consumers who are loyal to our service accustomed to the accuracy of our information. How do we attract more users? To save the profession, we must begin to forge new partnerships with students, faculty, campus organizations and service departments, and the general community. To do so we can, for example:

- Enlist the business world by working with interns, or creating a service hub for the business men and women of the community to enjoy.
- When conducting surveys or focus groups, enlist the assistance of grad students on campus.
- Reach out to the tutoring center and partner with them to reach more students.
- Remember special interest groups, such as student athletes, and create programs where they have an opportunity to enjoy special access to assisted library research and study skills sessions.
- Create faculty alliances by developing faculty centers, serving on faculty senates, and collaborating on research.
- Attend special events such as open houses, poetry readings, sporting events, and receptions.

New partnerships are formed organically. Congratulations for capturing new library user-groups!

According to Schuman (1990, p. 88), public relations are key to promoting the librarian. "It means coalition building, it means full participation in the intellectual and political life of campus and the community." She believes many people in the community are shocked to find out that librarians have Master's degrees, rather they generally hold librarians to an image reflected in appearances or popular culture. Schuman said "The image we worry about most—that of the middle-aged spinster librarian—is basically irrelevant and unimportant. What is important is the view of the library as foreboding, boring, complicated, largely inaccessible, or worse, irrelevant." How true is this concern today? Answer that question by surveying librarians as well as library constituents. She suggests we focus on how useful, necessary, and important we are to their education and research. We can strive to be considered the disseminators of information, instead of the guardians of knowledge.

We must use marketing principles to educate users about what we can do for them. First, let's gather data on what they want us to do, then do everything possible to project a more positive image. We are professionals, like doctors and nurses, who have dedicated years of coursework to become such. We strive for continual improvement and education. Professionals create partnerships with their client base. Academic librarians can partner not only with students, but with student groups, such as a class of psychology students who all seek memoirs to write a course paper. We can also partner also with open house coordinators, residence hall directors, student government groups, and faculty, for example.

9.8 Promote the five W's

Good customer service creates converts. Those students and faculty become our allies and partners on campus. Each experience with the library staff or facilities, whether on-campus or off-campus, needs to be a positive interaction. Barriers to good service must to be examined and studied. What impacts positivity? It's easy for the librarian to answer a question, perhaps obtaining a full-text article for the student. But why must the student need to ask for help in order to have a positive experience? Accessing full text for a library database is just straight-up difficult for the average patron. How hard must we actually make it before we realize they are giving up on us? They will move on to other resources.

Instead of reaching out for assistance, students are reaching for an easy to access Internet Web. Those who use library services such as reference or circulation desk assistance know what they need to ask. Users outside of this category normally do not know:

- *Who[m]* should they ask a question?
- *What* questions should they ask?
- *Why* are they asking a question?
- *When* should they ask?
- *Where* they should go to ask the question?

The secret is to convert nonusers to users using the principles of the five W's as part of the marketing plan. If good customer service, characterized by accuracy, speed, reliability, and accessibility, are a librarian's niche, then we must use the theory of the five W's to advertise to nonusers. For example, if the survey data shows users do not know what they should be asking, or whom to ask, the librarians can promote services through the use of educational flyers, school newspaper interviews, and in-library instruction sessions. In each forum, the librarians can specifically describe library services.

Library patrons really don't want to need help. They want the library to be as easy to use as the Internet so they can be independent researchers. We currently make them jump through three or four library platforms: sometimes from an Ebscohost interface, through to a ProQuest or Science Direct interface, through Serials Solutions or Link Source, to an abstract that may or may not have a link to full text somewhere on the page. Also, some results guide users to a library catalog record that merely indicates we have the needed item and that it's bound, on fiche, or in current periodicals. None of this makes sense to a novice. It might not even make sense to a seasoned library user. Library instruction has always been the librarian's answer to the problems of complexity in our systems. Perhaps the answer should be to spend more time on creating systems that are intuitive for researchers to use.

The most satisfied user-groups are likely the ones who have used an intervention method. They exhibit at least one competency from the five W's. A savvy professor or other satisfied classmate became a friend of library services because he or she knew whom or what to ask in time to complete an assignment. Students who are knowledgeable about the five W's may use a productive communication system, such as calling on the phone if off campus, or sending an email or text message. If these students are on campus, they stop by the desk for consultation regarding their complex research needs. In this positive experience, they encouraged other students to use library services and in effect, "paid it forward." Word of mouth is a fantastic method to increase a customer base. Good service breeds good experiences. On the flip side, customers will most often, when dissatisfied, complain to other customers, both users and nonusers.

9.9 Conclusion

The time is now. Marketing the profession is as important as marketing the library where you work. Although one helps improve the general image of the other, make a conscientious effort to consider and plan a marketing initiative for your librarians. Seek the buy-in that is necessary to make the plan more successful. The more librarians on board the better the team can steer the ship.

Librarians must become a team of engaged professionals dedicated to marketing not only the libraries where they work, but the profession in which they serve. As the twenty-first century presents challenges and opportunities, it impacts the life of our profession and our professional spaces. Take the methods discussed, to take our marketing plan and implementation process, to understand our own opportunities by using the heretofore systematic process of marketing in the realm of librarianship. Such opportunities as providing excellent customer service, becoming partners with other campus constituents, becoming a research expert and respected scholar, and using marketing principles to use a data driven approach to improve our image.

9.10 Exercises

1. Complete the following phrase: *The mission of a librarian is to...*
2. Complete the following phrase: *Our vision for the future is to...*
3. *SWOT*—add to the following example:

Internal forces	External forces
Strengths • Customer service oriented • Understand accuracy of information	Opportunities • Redesign interfaces so tools are easier to use • Market profession to improve image in the academic world and larger society
Weaknesses • Misunderstood professionally • Librarian-centric tools and services	Threats • Librarian-centric • Google Scholar and the rise of other easy to use Internet resources

4. This sample SWOT chart can be constructed by individual libraries. Each can look unique, but the skeleton will be the same. In what ways do you think the SWOT will remain consistent across all libraries?
5. List five questions to include in a faculty assessment survey of the library. List five questions to include on a student survey.

References

Abram, S. (1996). Marketing your valuable experience. *MLS (Marketing Library Services), 10*, 4–5.

Leiter, R. A. (2003). Reflections on Ranganathan's five laws of library science. *Law Library Journal, 95*, 411.

Mathews, B. (2009). *Marketing today's academic library*. Chicago: American Library Association, p. viii.

Schuman, P. G. (1990). The image of librarians: Substance or shadow? *Journal of Academic Librarianship, 16*, 86–89.

Siess, J. A. (2003). *The visible librarian: Asserting your value with marketing and advocacy*. Chicago: American Library Association.

Smith, D. (2011). Strategic marketing of library resources and services. *College and Undergraduate Libraries, 18*(4), 333–349.

Wysock, B. (2005). How Dr. Papadakis runs a university like a company. *The Wall Street Journal*. Retrieved from, http://online.wsj.com/news/articles/SB110912375606461666.

Conclusion

I didn't become a librarian to see my profession perish. I won't be phased out like a telephone operator or the neighborhood newspaper delivery boy. Still like many other professions, librarians are at risk. Consider the jobs of supermarket cashier or the mailman—each may see its demise. Do we want to be added to that list of professions to die? Should librarians become extinct, so will the institution of the library. Should libraries fail, so too will the profession. We must act. It is my intention to instill a new paradigm into our profession, to save what we love: our libraries. To save libraries is to save our profession, as one depends on the other.

The time is now…

- to discover
- to assess
- to plan
- to partner
- to promote
- to create our own destiny.

To *discover*, we must begin to reevaluate our mission, vision, and SWOT analysis. When we *assess*, we gather user-centric data to drive our improvement plans. To *plan* involves using project control principles to guide us through the market planning process. When we begin to act in *partnership* with our fellow librarians and in response to the needs of our constituents, we uncover opportunities, and create new or improve existing resources and services. Which services we choose depends on our organization. Do we need to increase usage of research consultation? Are e-books in our future? Can we increase turn-around time for ILL deliveries? So many questions and so many answers, waiting for us to discover, assess, and plan. When we act, we create *promotional* materials. *Promotions* come late in the game. We must remember that marketing is so much more than promoting; our marketing plan includes these data-driven discoveries, assessments, and mission planning. The promotional design process begins only at the end of this planning process. And we must remember that marketing plans are never completed because our reassessment of our services and our users' needs is continual. My approach to marketing is systematic, designed to bring success to libraries of all sizes and librarians of all skill levels.

The process I've outlined is assistive in creating marketing plans for librarians and the libraries where they work. This is critical if librarians are to survive and thrive. Remember that surviving basically describes our ability to maintain the status quo. But to thrive is to bring more prestige and awareness to our profession. We should not accept the mousy image thrust upon us in so much of popular culture. We need to stand tall and firm: libraries and librarians are critical to college campuses, to researchers, and to any individual seeking assistance in wading through oceans of information.

Technology drives our profession and in many ways, we are outsiders who take what technology offers. This is not in our best interest. We need to *partner* with those who create library resources, uncovering and developing opportunities to create library resources that are as easy to use as modern-day Internet resources like Google, Google Scholar, and Wikipedia.

Within these chapters, I've gathered information from a body of well-crafted literature. I conducted on-site consultations and presented case studies within these chapters. Additionally, I have incorporated practical methods to create and organize the roadmap to cultural success.

We began with a review of our history, the philosophies of the academic library's early thinkers, and a discussion of modern perspectives. Then we discussed planning for change, and the important assessment phases needed to determine what we must change and how—this is how we will market the twenty-first century library. We recognized the importance of partnering with other campus entities as we move forward. And we explored this new paradigm, including promoting the right resources and services, at the right time, to the right audiences, using the right methods –matching our twenty-first century challenges to the twenty-first century technologies at our disposal. Let's do it. Let's take a user-centric approach to improvements. Let's create our own destiny.

Suggested readings

Aharony, N. (2009). Librarians' attitudes towards marketing library services. *Journal of Librarianship and Information Science*, *41*(1), 39–50.
Angell, K. (2013). Open source assessment of academic library patron satisfaction. *Reference Services Review*, *41*(4), 593–604.
Archer, S. B. (2001). "Be all that you can be": Developing and marketing professionalism in academic reference librarianship. *The Reference Librarian*, *35*(73), 351–360.
Ashcroft, L. (2010). Marketing strategies for visibility. *Journal of Librarianship and Information Science*, *42*(2), 89–96.
Barile, L. (2011). Mobile technologies for libraries a list of mobile applications and resources for development. *College & Research Libraries News*, *72*(4), 222–228.
Battles, J., Glenn, V., & Shedd, L. (2011). Rethinking the library game: Creating an alternate reality with social media. *Journal of Web Librarianship*, *5*(2), 114–131.
Beck, S. E., & Manuel, K. (2008). *Practical research methods for librarians and information professionals*. New York, NY: Neal-Schuman Publishers.
Besant, L. X., & Sharp, D. (2000). Upsize this! Libraries need relationship marketing. *Information Outlook*, *4*(3), 17–18.
Betz, B., Brown, S. W., Barberi, D., & Langendorfer, J. M. (2009). Marketing library database services to end users: Peer-to-peer outreach using the Student Ambassador Program (SAm). *The Serials Librarian*, *56*(1–4), 250–254.
Brophy, P. (2007). *The library in the twenty-first century*. Library Assn Pub Ltd: Neal-Schuman.
Brunsdale, M. (2000). From mild to wild: Strategies for promoting academic libraries to undergraduates. *Reference & User Services Quarterly*, *39*(4), 331–335.
Carscaddon, L., & Chapman, K. (2013). Twitter as a marketing tool for libraries. In B. C. Thomsett-Scott (Ed.), *Marketing with social media: A LITA guide*. Chicago: American Library Association.
Charnigo, L., & Barnett-Ellis, P. (2013). Checking out Facebook.com: The impact of a digital trend on academic libraries. *Information Technology and Libraries*, *26*(1), 23–34.
Click, A., & Petit, J. (2010). Social networking and web 2.0 in information literacy. *The International Information & Library Review*, *42*(2), 137–142.
Connaway, L. S., & Powell, R. R. (2010). *Basic research methods for librarians*. Santa Barbara, CA: ABC-CLIO.
Cook, D., & Farmer, L. S. (2011). *Using qualitative methods in action research: How librarians can get to the why of data*. Chicago, IL: Association of College and Research Libraries.
Covey, D. T. (2005). Using data to persuade: State your case and prove it. *Library Leadership and Management*, *19*(2), 82–89.
Dewan, P. (2010). Why your academic library needs a popular reading collection now more than ever. *College & Undergraduate Libraries*, *17*(1), 44–64.
Duderstadt, J. J. (2009). Possible futures for the research library in the 21st century. *Journal of Library Administration*, *49*(3), 217–225.
Duke, L. M., & Tucker, T. (2007). How to develop a marketing plan for an academic library. *Technical Services Quarterly*, *25*(1), 51–68.
Estall, C., & Stephens, D. (2011). A study of the variables influencing academic library staff's attitudes toward marketing. *New Review of Academic Librarianship*, *17*(2), 185–208.

Farnum, C. M., Baird, C., & Ball, K. (2011). Can I make a suggestion? Your library suggestion box as an assessment tool. *Partnership: The Canadian Journal of Library and Information Practice and Research*, 6(1). Retrieved from: <http://davinci.lib.uoguelph.ca/index.php/perj/article/view/1431/2072>.

Feeney, M., & Sult, L. (2011). Project management in practice: Implementing a process to ensure accountability and success. *Journal of Library Administration*, 51(7–8), 744–763.

Fernandez, J. (2009). A SWOT analysis for social media in libraries. *Online*, 33(5), 35–37.

Franklin, B. (2012). Surviving to thriving: Advancing the institutional mission. *Journal of Library Administration*, 52(1), 94–107.

Gall, D. (2012). Librarian like a rock star: Using your personal brand to promote your services and reach distant users. *Journal of Library Administration*, 52(6–7), 549–558.

Gambles, B., & Schuster, H. (2003). The changing image of Birmingham libraries: Marketing strategy into action. *New Library World*, 104(9), 361–371.

Ganster, L., & Schumacher, B. (2009). Expanding beyond our library walls: Building an active online community through Facebook. *Journal of Web Librarianship*, 3(2), 111–128.

Gibson, C., & Mandernach, M. (2013). Reference service at an inflection point: Transformations in academic libraries. Retrieved from http://www.ala.org/acrl/sites/ala.org.acrl/files/content/conferences/confsandpreconfs/2013/papers/GibsonMandemach_Reference.pdf

Hallmark, E. K., Schwartz, L., & Roy, L. (2007). Developing a long-range and outreach plan for your academic library: The need for a marketing outreach plan. *College & Research Libraries News*, 68(2), 92–95.

Helinsky, Z. (2014). *A short-cut to marketing the library*. Amsterdam: Elsevier.

Hopkins, F. L. (1982). A century of bibliographic instruction: The historical claim to professional and academic legitimacy. *College and Research Libraries*, 43(3), 192–198.

Hossain, M. J., & Ahmed, S. Z. (2013). Developing a service performance assessment system to improve service quality of academic libraries. *Business Information Review*, 30(4), 210–221.

Houghton-Jan, S. (2007). Twenty steps to marketing your library online. *Journal of Web Librarianship*, 1(4), 81–90.

Jacobson, T. B. (2011). Facebook as a library tool: Perceived vs. actual use. *College & Research Libraries*, 72(1), 79–90.

Juntunen, A., Muhonen, A., Nygrén, U., & Saarti, J. (2013). Reinventing the academic library and its mission: Service design in three merged Finnish libraries. *Advances in Librarianship: Vol. 36.* (pp. 225–246).

Kasperek, S., Dorney, E., Williams, B., & O'Brien, M. (2011). A use of space: The unintended messages of academic library web sites. *Journal of Web Librarianship*, 5(3), 220–248.

Keller, J. (2008). Branding and marketing your library. *Public Libraries*, 47(5), 45–51.

Kies, C. N. (1987). *Marketing and public relations for libraries (no. 10)*. Metuchen, NJ: Scarecrow Press.

Kietzmann, J. H., Hermkens, K., McCarthy, I. P., & Silvestre, B. S. (2011). Social media? Get serious! Understanding the functional building blocks of social media. *Business Horizons*, 54(3), 241–251.

Krishnan, Y. (2011). Libraries and the mobile revolution. *Computers in Libraries*, 31(3), 6.

Luthmann, A. (2007). Librarians, professionalism and image: Stereotype and reality. *Library Review*, 56(9), 773–780.

Massey-Burzio, V. (1998). From the other side of the reference desk: A focus group study. *The Journal of Academic Librarianship*, 24(3), 208–215.

Mi, J., & Nesta, F. (2006). Marketing library services to the Net Generation. *Library Management*, 27(6/7), 411–422.

Miles, D. B. (2013). Shall we get rid of the reference desk? *Reference & User Services Quarterly*, 52(4), 320–333.

Nitecki, D. A. (2011). Space assessment as a venue for defining the academic library. *Library Quarterly: Information, Community, Policy*, 81(1), 27–59.

Parker, R., Kaufman-Scarborough, C., & Parker, J. C. (2007). Libraries in transition to a marketing orientation: Are librarians' attitudes a barrier? *International Journal of Nonprofit and Voluntary Sector Marketing*, 12(4), 320–337.

Patange, J. T. (2013). Marketing of library and information products and services. *GJHSS-G: Linguistics & Education*, 13(1), 33–36.

Polger, M. A., & Okamoto, K. (2013). Who's spinning the library? Responsibilities of academic librarians who promote. *Library Management*, 34(3), 236–253.

Pulliam, B., & Landry, C. (2010). Tag, you're it! Using QR codes to promote library services. *The Reference Librarian*, 52(1–2), 68–74.

Ramirez, M. L., & Miller, M. D. (2011). Approaches to marketing an institutional repository to campus, 13.

Rempel, H. G., Hussong-Christian, U., & Mellinger, M. (2011). Graduate student space and service needs: A recommendation for a cross-campus solution. *The Journal of Academic Librarianship*, 37(6), 480–487.

Robinson, C. K. (2012). Peter Drucker on marketing: Application and implications for libraries. *The Bottom Line: Managing Library Finances*, 25(1), 4–12.

Rogers, S. C. (2001). *Marketing strategies, tactics, and techniques: A handbook for practitioners*. Westport, Conn: Quorum Books.

Rowe, J., & Britz, J. J. (2009). Strategies for success: A framework for the development of a marketing plan for information services. *Mousaion*, 27(2), 36–50.

Russo, M. C., & Wootton Colborn, N. (2002). Something for (almost) nothing-public relations on a shoestring in an academic library. *Library Administration and Management*, 16(3), 138–145.

Sachs, D. E., Eckel, E. J., & Langan, K. A. (2011). Striking a balance: Effective use of Facebook in an academic library. *Internet Reference Services Quarterly*, 16(1–2), 35–54.

Salony, M. F. (1995). The history of bibliographic instruction: Changing trends from books to the electronic world. *The Reference Librarian*, 24(51–52), 31–51.

Seeholzer, J., & Salem, J. A. (2010). Library on the go: A focus group study of the mobile web and the academic library. *College & Research Libraries*, 72(1), 9–20.

Sokoloff, J. (2009). International libraries on Facebook. *Journal of Web Librarianship*, 3(1), 75–80.

Spalding, H. H., & Wang, J. (2006). The challenges and opportunities of marketing academic libraries in the USA: Experiences of US academic libraries with global application. *Library Management*, 27(6/7), 494–504.

Sump-Crethar, A. N. (2012). Making the most of Twitter. *The Reference Librarian*, 53(4), 349–354.

Thomas, L. C. (2010). Twitter at the office. *Journal of Web Librarianship*, 4(1), 79–82.

Thomas, L. C. (2011). Design for double rainbow. *Journal of Web Librarianship*, 5(1), 63–67.

Trott, B., & Elliott, J. (2007). Academic libraries and extracurricular reading promotion. *Reference & User Services Quarterly*, 46(3), 34–43.

Vasileiou, M., & Rowley, J. (2011). Marketing and promotion of e-books in academic libraries. *Journal of Documentation*, 67(4), 624–643.

Wakeham, M. (2004). Marketing and health libraries. *Health Information & Libraries Journal*, 21(4), 237–244.

Wood, E. J. (1983). Strategic planning and the marketing process: Library applications. *Journal of Academic Librarianship*, 9(1), 15–20.

Index

Note: Page numbers followed by *f* indicate figures *b* indicate boxes and *t* indicate tables.

A

Abram, S., 89
AcademicShare, 65
Action research, 19, 22–23
Administrators, 1–2, 10, 16–17, 24, 28, 32, 35, 36, 37, 42, 48, 51, 57, 58, 61
Advertising, 9–10, 11, 14, 17, 18, 32, 33, 54, 58–59, 67, 69, 70, 71, 75, 76, 80
Advocates, 51, 54, 66, 72, 76–77
Alumni, 16–17, 32, 51, 52
Amazon, 4, 75
Ambassadors, 48, 52, 54–56, 66
American Marketing Association (AMA), 3–4
Anonymity, 25
Applied research, 19
Appreciative inquiry, 47
Apprehension, 3–4
Article Linker, 1–2, 69
Assessment tools, 23–28, 32, 35, 37
Association of Research Libraries (ARL), 24, 31
Atwater-Singer, M., 61

B

Babaei, H.R., 77
Balloons, 8, 14, 76
Banned Book Week, 64
Barnes and Nobles, 75
Battles, J., 79
Beck, S.E., 28–29
Bellafante, N., 53. *See also* Drexel University
Bell, S., 78
Bias, 19–20, 24, 25, 27
Bibliographic instruction, 14–15, 18
Big data, 10
Bishop, C., 43
Blue Crew, 55*b*. *See also* University of Texas at San Antonio
Board members, 16–17, 32
Bookless libraries, 52, 55, 85

Books, 1–2, 3, 4–5, 7, 8, 9, 10, 13, 14, 15, 16–17, 25, 32, 49, 52, 55, 61, 64, 67, 68, 69–70, 71, 72, 75, 79, 82, 83, 85, 89, 90
 discussions, 64
 launching, 64
Branding, 8, 71–72
Bridges, M., 80
Brochures, 33, 70, 71–72
Bull, J., 47
Business model, 4, 31, 54

C

Campus newsletters/newspapers, 54
Captive audience, 9, 15, 32, 75–76, 77, 78, 82, 83, 87
Carolyn Cunningham, 55. *See also* University of Texas at San Antonio
Cassell, K.A., 51
2014 Celebration of Recently Published Faculty Authors, 62. *See also* Rutgers University
Change management, 46–48
Chow, A.S., 80–81
Circulation desk, 92
Citation management systems, 58
Code of Federal Regulations, Section 46, Title 45, 29
Collaboration, 51, 57–58, 60, 61
Collection development, 37*t*, 58, 61
Collection management, 58, 60
Comfort zone, 2, 47, 64
Commander, P., 80
Computer mediated communication (CMC), 27
Connaway, L.S., 23, 24, 25, 27
Connell, R.S., 80, 82
Consortium of Academic and Research Librarians in Illinois (CARLI), 83
Constituent, 1–2, 4–5, 8, 16, 17, 29, 31, 32, 33, 34, 35, 36, 38, 48, 51, 52–56, 66, 67, 68, 70, 72, 76–77, 80–81, 86, 88–89, 90–91, 92, 93, ix, x, 95

Cook, D
Cooperrider, D.L., 47–48
Course management software, 70, 71
Covey, D.T., 37
Customer service, 10, 11, 13–14, 27, 69–71, 73, 87, 88–90, 92–93, 94*t*

D

Dana, J.C., 10–11, 15, 17, 55–56, 69–70, x
Direct selling, 70–71
Discovery tools, 2, 7, 8, 69, 75, 82, 90
Displays, ix, ix, 14, 55, 79
Document delivery, 42, 43–44, 48, 59, 71
Drexel University
  Bellafante, N., 53
  Hagerty Library, 52
  Nitecki, D. PhD, 52
  Papadakis, C.D. Dr., 85
  Ten Have, B., 53
Drury, F.K.W., 13–14, 15, x
Dubicki, E., 67, 70, 72
D'Youville College Upward Bound program, 48, 65

E

EBooks, 1–2
Ebscohost, 69, 75, 82, 93
Events, 7, 8, 9, 15, 17, 19, 33, 41, 42, 54–55, 58, 61–62, 64, 66, 71, 76–77, 79, 82, 83, 91
Executive summary, 31, 34, 35, 37
Exhibits, 11, 25, 62, 82, 93

F

Facebook, 24, 25, 54, 72, 76, 77, 79, 82–83, 85–86, 87
Facilitator, 32
Faculty, 1–2, 7, 10, 13, 16, 21, 27, 32, 35, 41, 51, 52, 54, 57–60, 61–62, 65, 66, 70–71, 75–76, 78, 85, 87, 90, 91, 92, 94
  council, 58
  events, 58, 61–62, 71
  senate, 58, 91
Farmer, L., 21–22
Fisk, J., 72
Five W's, 87, 92–93
Flyers, 8, 9–10, 11, 34, 76, 92–93, x

Focus group, 2, 3–4, 9, 15, 19, 20, 21, 23, 25–28, 26*t*, 29, 32, 33, 36, 38, 43, 57–58, 76, 91
Four P's of Marketing, 32

G

Gantt chart, 37, 44, 45*f*
Get it for me, 71
Giveaways, 72, 76
Glazer, H., 62. *See also* Rutgers University
Glen, V., 79
Global impact, 64
Google, 7, 8, 9, 15, 16, 37, 37*t*, 59–60, 68, 69, 75, 82, 85–86, 87, 88, 96
Google books, 7
Google Help-outs, 87, 88
Google Scholar, 4, 7, 9, 15, 37*t*, 59–60, 68, 69–70, 75, 82, 85–86, 87, 94*t*, 96
Green, S.S., 10, 15, 17, x
Gupta, D.K., 31
Guttenberg, J., 7

H

Hagerty Library, 52. *See also* Drexel University
Hathi Trust, 7, 69
Helinsky, Z., 31
Hidden market, 75–76
Hiremath, U., 51
History, 4–5, 9–10, 13, 48, 68–69, x, 96
Hold shelf, 11
House calls, 58–59

I

ILLiad, 5, 48, 60
Image, 4, 11, 34, 51, 57, 79, 86, 87, 89, 91, 92, 93, 94*t*, 95–96
Implementation schedule, 33, 35, 37
Information literacy, 7, 17, 61, 64, 79, 88, 91
Initiatives, 2, 5, 23, 41–49, 52, 55–56, 70, 79, 93
In-servicing, 21, 41, 58–59, 60, 75–76
Instant Messaging (IM), 61
Institutional review board (IRB), 19, 29
Interdepartmental partnerships, 61
Interlibrary loan, 7, 13, 25, 28, 32, 37*t*, 48, 49, 54, 68, 70–71, 80–81, 89

Internet, 4–5, 7, 9, 14, 15, 17, 27, 32, 67, 68, 69–70, 76, 77–78, 79, 80, 87, 88–89, 90, 92, 93, 94t, ix, 96
Internet searching, 59–60
Interview, 9, 15, 19–20, 23, 25–28, 29, 49, 51, 52, 53, 57–58, 62, 72, 76, 91, 92–93, x
Interviewer objectivity, 27

J

Jasse, L., 55. *See also* University of Texas at San Antonio
John Cotton Dana public relations award, 55, 56. *See also* Dana, J.C.

K

Kaur, K., 75, 77–78
Keller, J.R., 44
Kelly, T., 46, 47
Kilzer, R., 53
Knowledge transfer, 64
Koontz, C., 67, 72
Kotter, W., 57–58

L

Leiter, R.A., 13, 88
Leong, J.H.T., 64
LibQUAL+, 24
Librarian-centric, 82, 94t, x
Librarian-to-librarian partnerships, 61
Librarian-to-staff partnerships, 61
Library as space, x
Library instruction, 5, 17, 33, 37t, 58, 59, 71, 75–76, 78, 79, 93
Likert scale, 21
Lubans, J., 47
Lucas, D., 41–42, 44, 48–49, 58–59, 65

M

Maloney, K. PhD, 55. *See also* University of Texas at San Antonio
Marketing/project portfolio, 42
Market planning, 5, 8, 9, 13, 17, 31, 32, 35, 37, xi, 95
Market research, 32
Market researcher (MR), 26–27
Mathews, B., 54, 87

Mill, H., 85
Mission statement, 8, 11, 33, 34, 35–36, 44, 49, 64, 87
Mobile apps, 80–82
Moderator, 25–27, 32
Murphy, S.A., 31, 32

N

National Institute of Health, 7
Newsletters, 11, 33, 54–55, 70, 72
Newspaper articles, 9–10, 11, 54, 59
Nitecki, D. PhD, 52. *See also* Drexel University

O

Obeidy, W.K., 77
OCLC Perceptions of Libraries 2010, 69–70
Online Computer Library Center (OCLC), 68, 69–70, 71, 72, 76, 81
Online databases, 16, 59–60, 68, 71, 80–81
Online games, 79
Open houses, 54–55, 70, 71, 91, 92
Open source software, 7
Outreach, 33, 58, 64, 65, 87

P

Pamphlets, 11
Papadakis, C. PhD, 85. *See also* Drexel University
Partnering opportunities and constituencies (POC), 52, 57–58, 61–62
Partnership, x, x, 5, 10, 47–48, 51, 52–56, 57–60, 61–62, 64–65, 66
Peer coaches, 55. *See also* University of Texas at San Antonio
Pena, D., 10
Personal narrative, 26
Peters, A., 55–56. *See also* University of Texas at San Antonio
Phillips, N.K., 83
Pinterest, 72, 78–79
Posters, 2, 11, 34, 70, 71–72
Powell, R.R., 23, 24, 25, 27
Preservation, 58, 60, 64, 90
Pretesting, 24
Printing press, 7, 17

Print resources, 59
Project champion, 44. *See also* Project management
Project charter, 43. *See also* Project management
Project control, 5, 41–49. *See also* Project management
Project management
　project champion, 44
　project charter, 43
　project control, 5, 41–49
　project manager, 41, 42, 43–44, 47–48
　project portfolio (*see* Marketing/project portfolio)
　project sponsor, 47–48, 49
Project Manager, 41, 42, 43–44, 47–48. *See also* Project management
Project portfolio, 42. *See also* Project management
Project sponsor, 47–48, 49. *See also* Project management
Promotion, x, x, x, 2, 3, 5, 9, 14, 17, 21–22, 31, 32, 67, 71, 72, 75–76, 77, 86, 90, 95
Promotional tools
　balloons, 76
　book bags, 72
　book marks, 72
　brochures, 33, 71–72
　campus newsletters/newspapers, 54
　can cozies, 72
　displays, 62
　exhibits, 11, 25, 62, 82, 93
　folders, 72
　giveaways, 72, 76
　newsletters, 11, 33, 54–55, 70, 72
　newspaper articles, 9–10, 11, 54, 59
　notepads, 72
　pencils pens, 72
　posters, 2, 11, 34, 70, 71–72
　post-its, 72
　staplers, 72
　water bottles, 72
ProQuest, 75, 82, 93
ProQuest flow, 58
Publicity, 10, 13–14, 32, 36, 69–70, 77–78
Publishing, 33
PubMed, 4, 60

Q

Qualitative research, 20, 21, 29
Quantitative research, 20, 21–22
QWERTY keyboard, 85

R

Radford, M., 22–23
Ranganathan, S.R., 13, 15
Reactive marketing, 8
Reader advisories, 14
Reassess, 5, 37, 46
Recruiting, 52, 54–55
Reference desk. *See* Research desk
Renberg, G., 9–10
Research assistance, 11, 13–14, 59, 60
Research desk, 2, 13–14, 21, 28–29, 54, 59, 70–71, 78
Research guides, 70
Research method, 19, 20, 21, 22, 28–29, 58, 91
Reserves/e-Reserves, 13, 70–71
Response rate, 25, 27, 29
Roach, M., 25
RSS feeds, 70
RUSA, 51
Rutgers University
　2014 Celebration of Recently Published Faculty Authors, 62
　Glazer, H., 62
Ryan, B., 81

S

Sample size, 20, 24, 25
Sauermann, H., 30
Savard, R., 31
Schneider, T., 65
Schuman, P.G., 92
Siess, J.A., 88
Serial solutions, 1–2, 69, 93
Shareholders, 43
Shedd, L., 79
Sherrill, K., 61
Shoaf, E.C., 26–27
Siess, J.A., 88–89
Slogans, 72
Smartphone, 85–86
Smith, D., 87
Social media, 8, 16–17, 76–77, 79

Social networking sites (SNS), 72
Social networks, 77
Somani, S., 47
Special events, 71
Speeches, 11
Statistical significance, 20, 25, 29
Strategic planning, 8, 33
Students, 1–2, 3, 5, 7, 8, 9, 10, 14, 15, 16, 17, 21, 24, 25–26, 28–29, 32, 33, 35, 43–44, 48, 49, 51, 52–53, 54–55, 56, 57, 58–60, 61–62, 65, 67, 68, 69–71, 72, 75, 78, 80–81, 83, 85, 86, 89, 90, 91, 92, 93, ix
Summey, T.P., 34, 72
Summon, 1–2, 4, 8, 69
Survey
 Monkey, 23, 24
 pool, 21, 28
Survivor Day, 64
SWOT, 5, 33, 34, 36–37, 37t, 42, 67, 68, 87, 88, 90–91, x, 95
Systematic review, 20

T

Targeted emails, 70, 80
Ten Have, B. *See* Drexel University
Texas A&M, 71
Think, Investigate, Plan, React (TIPR), 4, 5, 21–22, 23, 75, 86, 91–92, x
Thomas, L.C., 77
Thornton, E., 78–79
Trustees, 2, 16–17, 35–36
Turry, P., 85
Tutorials, 17, 83
Twenty-first Century, 1, 2, 3–4, 5, 7, 8, 9, 10, 13, 14, 16, 17, 23, 37t, 38, 41, 47–48, 52, 55–56, 69, 82, 85–86, 87, 90, 91, 93, x, xi, 96
Twitter, 24, 25, 54, 72, 77, 78, 79, 85–86, 87
Typewriter, 85

U

University of Alabama, 79
University of Texas at San Antonio (UTSA)
 Blue Crew, 55b

Cunningham, C., 55
Maloney, K. PhD, 55
Peer coaches, 55
Peters, A., 55–56
Usability studies, 81
User-centric, 1, 2, 28, 67, 82, 95, 96

V

Valentine, B., 25–26
Validity, 20, 25
Vinopal, J., 42
Virtual reference service, 42, 44, 88
Visible market, 75–77, 78
Vision statement, 3, 8, 34, 35–36, 38, 42, 67, 87, 90–91, x

W

Wang, J., 99
Webb, S., 43–44
Webmaster, 80
Website, 80–82
Website Messages, 80–81
Weeding, 13, 58, 60
Wenhong, J., 80
Whang, M., 75, 80–81
Wikipedia, 68, 96
Windsor, J., 15, 85
Wong, Z., 46
Word of mouth, 42, 43, 61, 69–71, 93
Workshops, 58, 70, 71
WorldCat, 69
Wysock, B., 85

Y

Yang, Z.Y.L, 58
Yazdanifard, R., 77
Yusoff, W.F.W., 77

Z

Zauha, J.M., 14
Zedeck, S., 19
Zhang, Y., 43